Praise for the book

I applaud Dr Bill Gent for the ground-breaking research on Hifz that he has carried out with great integrity and objectivity. He has described the facts as he saw them, without any prior agenda, and captured the world-view of the participants in their own words. I got to provide feedback on some of Dr Gent's articles published since the original ethnographic study and I always found him to be accommodating and genuinely interested in learning from different perspectives. As I already work in the Madrasah setting and know what it is like from the 'inside', I am particularly attracted by the copious Endnotes which bring the work up to date following subsequent research by the author and others. At a time when there is widespread misunderstanding of what actually takes place in an Islamic educational setting in modern-day Britain, this invaluable work will not only provide genuine insight but also provoke others to undertake similar ethnographic research.

Hafiz Abdullah Muhammad
Muslim scholar, author and teacher

This is an important piece of research that brings understanding to a form of religious education that many people have very little knowledge about: the memorization and recitation of the Qur'an. It helps us to realize the embodied nature of the Qur'an and the deep feelings of sincerity and commitment felt by those who have memorized it. Most Muslim children who take part of this type of Islamic supplementary education also attend secular school. This piece of research is therefore of relevance not only for those interested in the world of religions and religious education. It is also of interest and relevance to all types of school teachers and teacher students since many of their pupils might very well have the experience of a dual education where they move between secular education and the type of Islamic education described by Bill Gent. His ethnographic work brings forward diverse aspects of a tradition of Muslim learning that dates back to the very beginning of Islam, by many called the very 'back bone' of Islamic education.

Professor Jenny Berglund
Stockholm University, Stockholm

Given the wider and topically controversial arena concerning the integration of Muslim children and the role of Muslim educational institutions in the western world, this monograph, based on empirical research into the world of Qur'an memorisers within the British Muslim community, is indispensable. The reader cannot help but appreciate the wealth of educational knowledge and decades of teaching experience that accompanies Bill Gent in this book. Ideally positioned to conduct this fieldwork, Bill Gent successfully sheds light on the contexts, content and pedagogy of Qur'an education with a British Muslim community. Exploring the fascinating voices of young Muslim memorisers, he leaves us lingering with a deep appreciation for this over a thousand year old tradition by providing intimate insights into their experiences, dedication and sacrifices that are often understated, misunderstood or unknown by westerners. To those with an interest in European Islamic education or religious education in general, this monograph is a must-have and constitutes one of the few works available that is based on fieldwork within contemporary Islamic education institutions.

Dr Youcef Sai
Assistant Professor (Adjunct) of Islamic Studies
Department of Religions and Theology, Trinity College
Dublin, Ireland

Bill Gent is to be congratulated on a landmark publication. It opens up a little-explored world of Muslim education and suggests its significance to education more generally. Bill's data result from his consistently respectful and sensitive interaction with local Muslims and with Islamic tradition. For years I have been drawing his superb, pioneering research to the attention of educationists, ethnographic researchers and all who are interested in the dynamics of living Islam in the West. This timely publication brings Bill's work to a wider public at a time when intercultural understanding is so urgently needed.

Professor Eleanor Nesbitt
Professor Emeritus, University of Warwick

Bill Gent's monograph offers a rich ethnographic tapestry of the lived reality of Muslim supplementary education in Britain. The sensitive and sympathetic approach he adopts towards these often misunderstood traditional learning institutions overcomes, in a unique way, the challenges of an insider/outsider binary experienced by the researchers. His work makes a timely and significant contribution to the growing body of empirical studies in Islamic Education.

Dr Abdullah Sahin
Reader in Islamic Education
Warwick Religions and Education Research Unit
University of Warwick

Bill Gent's sensitively conducted ethnographic research in a British elementary mosque school provides an important corrective to popular conceptions of Islamic education. In addition to his compelling accounts of learning in an Islamic context, he illustrates how learning in Muslim supplementary schools can be complementary to learning through an inclusive, impartial education about religions in state-funded schools.

Professor Robert Jackson
Professor Emeritus, University of Warwick

MUSLIM SUPPLEMENTARY CLASSES

First published in the UK by Beacon Books and Media Ltd
Innospace, Chester Street, Manchester M1 5GD, UK.

In association with The Foundation for the Advancement of Muslim Education
www.thefame.org.uk

Copyright © William A. Gent 2018

The right of William A. Gent to be identified as the author of this work has been asserted in accordance with the Copyright, Designs and Patents Act 1988. All rights reserved. This book may not be reproduced, scanned, transmitted or distributed in any printed or electronic form or by any means without the prior written permission from the copyright owner, except in the case of brief quotations embedded in critical reviews and other non-commercial uses permitted by copyright law.

First paperback edition published 2018
Printed in the UK
www.beaconbooks.net

Cataloging-in-Publication record for this book is available from the British Library

ISBN 978-1-912356-15-7

Cover design by Bipin Mistry
Photographs © Imam Haroon Rashid Patel

MUSLIM SUPPLEMENTARY CLASSES

and their place within the wider learning community

A Redbridge-based study

Bill Gent

Contents

Foreword	xiii
Preface	xv
Overview	xix
Acknowledgements	xxi

1	***The Context and Timeliness of this Research***	1
1.1	Introduction	1
1.2	Professional encounters and opportunities: An autobiographical account	2
1.3	The historical roots of the British Muslim community	5
1.4	Redbridge and its Muslim community	7
1.5	The growing public interest in emergent British Islam	9
1.6	The continuing debate about the efficacy of traditional Islamic education	12
1.7	The increasing use of networking within the educational community	16
1.8	The growing official recognition of the contribution made by supplementary schooling	18
2	***Literature Review***	21
2.1	Introduction	21
2.2	Knowledge, learning and education in Islam	22
2.3	The culture of traditional Islamic education and learning	26
2.4	Hearing, learning and reciting the Qur'an	30
2.5	British Islam	36
2.6	Muslim educational life in Britain	39
2.7	A note on cyber Islam	41

3	*Methodology*	43
3.1	Introduction	43
3.2	Ethnography, reflexivity and the research diary	43
3.3	Life-story interviews	47
3.4	Two phases of research at Balfour Road Mosque	51
3.5	Fieldwork with a hifz class	52
3.6	Photography as a research tool	55
3.7	The monitoring of radio and television programmes	56

4	*Case Study One: Life-story Images of Muslim Education*	57
4.1	Introduction	57
4.2	The sample group	58
4.3	The lasting influence of a teacher	59
4.4	Episodes on the path of Qur'anic learning	61
4.5	The sub-culture of mosque-based education	62
4.6	Darker reminiscences of mosque-based education	64
4.7	The contested nature of traditional Islamic education	65

5	*Case Study Two: The Life and Work of Balfour Road Maktab*	69
5.1	Introduction	69
5.2	The origins, nature and premises of the community	70
5.3	Maktab students and teachers	71
5.4	Organisation of teaching and learning	73
5.5	Curriculum material and approaches	75

6	*Case Study Three: The Experience of Hifz Students at Balfour Road Maktab*	79
6.1	Introduction	79
6.2	The make-up of the target group	81
6.3	Routes into the hifz class	82
6.4	The routines and rhythms of the hifz class	85
6.5	The students' perceptions of what they were doing	88
6.6	The 'sacrifice' of becoming a hafiz	91
6.7	Hifz class and the rest of the students' lives	93

7	*Muslim Supplementary Classes Within the Wider Social and Educational Community*	95
7.1	Introduction	95
7.2	The value of Muslim supplementary classes as 'capital'	96
7.3	Muslim supplementary classes within the wider educational community	101
7.4	The place of memorisation in learning	104
7.5	Barriers and pathways to development	108
8	***Overview, Conclusions and Recommendations***	115
8.1	Introduction	115
8.2	Overview and conclusions	115
8.3	Areas for future research	121
8.4	Recommendations	122

Glossary of Non-English Terms Used in the Text	125
Endnotes and Commentary	133
References	149
Appendices	163
Appendix 1	163
Appendix 2	164
Appendix 3	165
Appendix 4	167
Appendix 5	168
Appendix 6	169
Appendix 7	170

Foreword

I am delighted to commend this important monograph as one of the most significant pieces of ethnographic research about Muslims in Britain of recent decades. Ever since I had the privilege of examining the professional doctoral thesis upon which this book is based back in 2006, I have advised my postgraduate students to use Bill Gent's work as a 'model' for how to undertake ethnography within a British Muslim institution with integrity, sensitivity, and academic rigour, and in spirit of collaboration and mutuality. Bill Gent allied his many years of professional experience in education with the world class expertise of the staff at the Warwick Religions and Education Research Unit at Warwick University. This winning combination resulted in a piece of research that reflects ethnographic practice at its best, and speaks to a broad range of disciplines. Educationalists, sociologists and anthropologists of religion, and Muslim leadership in its diverse forms, will find their understanding of a distinctive and time-honoured tradition of Muslim learning illuminated through Bill's carefully crafted writing.

The important findings of the research upon which this book is based rest upon sound and careful methodology. For example, allowing interviewees to choose their own pseudonym in order to maintain anonymity and confidentiality–rather than imposing a name upon them as is common in much ethnographic work–was an imaginative step in building relationships of trust and respect. Although Bill Gent's doctoral studies were undertaken some years ago and his findings embedded in the academic sources of the time, there is nonetheless a timelessness in his findings. This is partly due to the nature and historicity of the institution he explored; the practice of memorisation of the Qur'an stretches back to the very earliest days of Islam, and will undoubtedly continue to be an intrinsic and fundamental dimension of Muslim religious life in the future. Grounding his study within an appreciation of this tradition, and yet exploring it through the methods of current social scientific research, enables the reader to understand a historic tradition in its contemporary guise. Moreover, Bill Gent has continued to remain research-active in relation to the subject of British Muslim supplementary education, thereby offering us the benefit of his ongoing insights and perspectives.

Given the relative lack of research on the subject of Muslim supplementary schools in Britain, Bill Gent's work is of enormous significance. Through his work we meet some extraordinary young British Muslims who voluntarily commit themselves to a form of learning and self-discipline that would challenge those twice their age. We begin to appreciate the embodied nature of the Qur'an and the sense of responsibility felt by those who have memorised it, namely, to reflect the virtues commended in the Qur'an, and the example of the Prophet Muhammad to whom it was revealed.

Professor Sophie Gilliat-Ray
Director, Centre for the Study of Islam in the UK
Cardiff University

Preface

I was delighted to learn in the years following the completion of my Doctorate of Education thesis for the University of Warwick in May 2006 that the product of my research was being read and commented on positively. Indeed, I was flattered to learn that the thesis, and several other pieces of my work which I had published subsequently, had even been brought together to form a coursework exercise in one university's MA in Islamic Studies course.

Others who have trodden a similar academic path will undoubtedly have shared the mixed feelings that I experienced upon finishing the thesis: 'mixed' in that it involved both a feeling of elation upon completing (and surviving!) the exercise but also a feeling of lethargy as a natural consequence of all the time, life-focus and energy—physical and nervous—that had been expended on the project over a number of years. And that's not to mention, of course, the impact on family, friends and life style.

Following the award of the degree, a further issue began to emerge: should I let the research and reading in the field in which I had been researching now drop so that I could move on to other projects and activities? (Could I pick up once again, for instance, my life-long interest in paremiology—the study of proverbs?) But my growing interest in the whole field of Islamic education, which encompassed so many other related fields (including schooling, pedagogy, Qur'anic studies, and epistemology) was such that it would not let me drop it! So, after a short break, I resumed my background reading, attendance at conferences and other gatherings, giving talks and writing papers, and getting published some aspects of that which I had researched (see, for example: Gent 2005, 2006, 2011a, 2011b, 2013) but increasingly drawing in knowledge and insights from later study and exploration (see, for example, Gent 2015, 2018 [in press]).

So, as a matter of course almost, new horizons began to appear, sometimes the result of the accumulation of new knowledge and insights but, at other times, as the result of chance encounters and meetings. As an example of the latter, I remember so clearly attending a course at Chester University when a Muslim scholar sitting next to me and with whom I had been chatting said, almost as an aside, 'Oh, have you read *The Storyteller of Jerusalem* about the life and times of Wasif Jawhariyyeh?' I hadn't but, upon return home, one of my first tasks was to order and then read this fascinating book which not only fed my love of biographical writing but also my knowledge of life in a particular culturally mixed society—that of Palestine from the beginning of the twentieth century to the founding of the state of Israel in 1948.

And running alongside these general developments was the growing conviction that I needed to build on the research that I had already carried out (mainly, of course, related to Muslim supplementary education and the hifz process). There was the niggling realisation that, for example, though it was possible to see hifz as the end of a process (that is, committing the entire Arabic Qur'an to memory), it was also very substantially the beginning of another: the commitment, for example, to keeping the memorised Qur'an 'alive' so that one could fulfil those duties expected of huffaz within a Muslim community. And then, given the profound linkage of knowledge and lifestyle/adab within the Muslim world-view, there was also the issue of what quality of life a hafiz or hafiza was expected to live. I began to see with growing realisation, that—as one of my original cohort of hifz class students had remarked to me—'You can't retire as a hafiz!'

And so, in consultation with my colleagues at the University of Warwick, I set up another research exercise into the lifestyle and expectations of huffaz within contemporary British society, the outcomes of which were condensed in an article *The Hidden Olympians: the role of huffaz in the English community* (Gent 2016). As ever, for me the thrill of such a research project lay not only in gaining new knowledge and in uncovering layers of meaning, but also in the conversations with a number of huffaz up and down the country: the heart of the ethnographic method, of course.

There was also another issue that tugged away at me: indeed, one that I had verbalised within the second of the recommendations that I had appended to the original thesis: for those Muslim children and young people to whom it applied, what impact does their attendance both at sites of Muslim learning (such as mosque supplementary classes) and secular state school have on the overall learning? Did they feel that engaging in both traditions of learning added to their quality of life? Would they want their own children to go through the same process? As I began to look more deeply into these issues—always with the setting up of another research project in mind—I was lucky enough to link up with a number of European colleagues who were thinking along the same lines. Indeed, as I write, Jenny Berglund (Professor of Religious Education at Stockholm University), and I are writing up for publication the results of a research project that she and I carried out in 2016 amongst a group of Muslim students at a large high school in Outer London. A further similar piece of research, but with older primary school Muslim pupils, is already underway.

And, whilst reflecting on the larger European scene, it is now also clear that the kind of work described above has a bearing on the field of European inter-cultural education that people like Professor Robert

Jackson have spearheaded and been developing in their ground-breaking work for the Council of Europe (see Council of Europe 2014).

Now, all this has a bearing on this book for, though the publisher and I wanted it to be in substance the original 2006 doctoral thesis, we also agreed that it would be foolish to ignore the fruits of my own and other people's work since. We decided that, rather than changing or adding to the text radically (though some editing would be needed), we would instead use the device of annotated endnotes as a means of commenting, and in many cases expanding on, the original text. For readers, then, we hope that the substantial section of endnotes that comes towards the end of this book will be of both general interest and academic value.

Bill Gent, Frinton-on-Sea, July 2018

Overview

Using his own professional experiences and fieldwork in the northeast of London as a starting point, the author suggests that the time is now right to consider the place of Muslim supplementary education in a wider social and educational setting. He suggests that four factors support this: the growing public interest in the emergence of British Islam; the continuing debate about the efficacy of traditional forms of Islamic education; the increasing use of networking within the educational community; and the growing official recognition of the contribution made by supplementary schooling.

Following a review of a wide range of relevant literary material, the author draws on a number of life-story interviews in order to portray the reality and variety of British Muslims' experience of Islamic education. The outcomes of ethnographic fieldwork are then used to describe and analyse what takes place in a British *maktab* (elementary mosque school). This includes a detailed explanation of how and why the Qur'an is learned, particularly by those individuals who are training to become *huffaz* (those who have committed the whole Qur'an to memory).

The ways in which Muslim supplementary schools might form part of the wider social and educational community are then explored together with factors that might block or encourage the creation of such an ideal. Analysis includes a review of existing organisational attempts to promote the work of supplementary schooling. A case is also presented for the re-appraisal of the role of memorisation as a distinct form of learning.

The thesis ends with a concluding statement, focusing on the ideal of *maktabs* and mainstream LEA schools working together to mutual benefit, and a number of recommendations aimed at researchers and those involved in both Muslim and wider community schooling.

Non-English words are listed in the glossary and are italicised in the text only on their first occurrence.

During the course of writing this thesis, changes in national and local government led to the replacement of the term 'local education authority' (LEA) with 'local authority' (LA). The use of one or the other term in the text depends upon the context.

Acknowledgements

In 2006, I thanked the following people for their help, support and encouragement: Eleanor Nesbitt (my doctoral supervisor whose wise and enlightened counsel helped me to set the course through the ups and downs of the initial research work), Haroon Patel (imam of Balfour Road Mosque, Ilford, who acted as gatekeeper for me into his mosque-community and its educational work), and my wife, Lynn (whose patience, common-sense and forbearance were beyond what I could ever have expected). I would like to acknowledge the assistance of my friend and colleague, Hafiz Abdullah Mohammad, in checking the draft of the glossary in order to correct errors and to offer guidance.

In relation to my work over recent years I would like, to thank, in addition: colleagues attached to the Warwick Religions and Educatio Research Unit (WRERU) at the University of Warwick for their support and fellowship, those many Muslim scholars and leaders who have given me their time with such innate humility; and the growing body of European scholars with which I am working for their eager collaboration and good-humoured friendship.

Bill Gent, August 2018

1 The Context and Timeliness of This Research

1.1 Introduction

At the beginning of this research exercise, two research questions, an aim, and a number of objectives were formulated.

The research questions were: What do Muslim students gain from their experiences in supplementary classes? and What is the potential contribution of Muslim supplementary classes to the wider educational community?

The aim was stated thus: From an understanding of what already happens in mosque classes, to explore ways in which Muslim supplementary classes might achieve a symbiotic relationship with the wider educational/learning community.

Six objectives were identified: to identify contemporary factors that make these research questions important; to explore the ways in which Muslim supplementary classes add value to the lives of their students; to explore contemporary critiques of Muslim supplementary classes in Britain; to identify those factors that might encourage or block a symbiotic relationship with the wider educational community from developing; to identify the consonance between such a symbiotic relationship and the idea of a 'learning community'; and, to make recommendations about how Muslim supplementary classes and mainstream schools might work together for mutual benefit.

The purpose of this opening chapter is to set the context of the research project as well as to demonstrate why it was an appropriate time to have conducted it.

The context of the research is outlined in the next three sections: an autobiographical account of the professional backdrop to the research (1.2); a brief historical survey of the growing Muslim presence in Britain (1.3); and, information about the London Borough of Redbridge and its Muslim population (1.4).

The remaining four sections set out a case for the timeliness of this research: the growing public interest in emergent British Islam (1.5); the continuing debate about the efficacy of traditional Islamic education (1.6); the increasing use of networking within the educational community as a whole (1.7); and, the growing official recognition of the contribution made by supplementary schooling (1.8).

1.2 Professional encounters and opportunities: An autobiographical account

As local authority adviser with responsibility for religious education in the London Borough of Redbridge (1988–2008), I developed contacts with a wide variety of religious and cultural groups. In 2000, however, my interest in the local Muslim community and the educational dimension of its life sharpened.

Having been approached by the local Child Protection Team (CPT) to assist in the production of a booklet for professionals working in a multi-cultural setting, I was asked by its members about how best to respond to occasional child protection complaints relating to 'mosque schools'. It became clear that team members were unclear on a number of counts: what 'mosque schools' were and how they operated, what leadership existed within the Muslim community, and how to make contacts without breaching religious and cultural protocols, customs and courtesies.

My response was to suggest the setting up what was loosely called an 'LEA/Mosque Schools' working group. This would bring together local Muslim leaders with links to mosque schools and local authority officers, notably members of the CPT. Once relationships had been made and trust established, I conjectured, there would exist the appropriate setting in which to discuss the kinds of issues that had stalled and baffled CPT members over many years.

The idea having been accepted, the 'LEA/Mosque Schools' working group, consisting of male Muslim leaders but both male and female local authority representatives, held its inaugural meeting in November 2001. The venue, significantly, was Ilford Islamic Centre and Mosque.

The conjecture proved sound in that, through a series of meetings, trusting relationships were established and 'sensitive' issues relating to child protection in mosque schools were broached, explored and discussed. Running parallel with this was discussion about Redbridge mosque schools in general: their number, location, organisation, curricula and styles of working.

But, once the novelty of the first few meetings was over, the issue arose of how best to continue the momentum and productivity of the group. At this stage, it was suggested that a text on mosque schools in Redbridge be produced for distribution amongst both mosque and LEA schools. As well as clarifying a range of issues, creating the text would in itself provide a focal point for the work of the group. Furthermore, the text itself would not only be a means of disseminating accurate information about the mosque school system but would also be a practical demonstration of collaboration between the Muslim and wider educational community.

And so the work on the text of what was eventually published as the booklet *Muslim Madrasahs in Redbridge* (Redbridge SACRE 2003) began. The dynamic of production was iterative; that is, a cumulative process was adopted through which text was drafted, discussed, amended and then new text added, the process repeating itself until the document had been completed to everyone's satisfaction.

The process of drafting text was not easy, however, for it meant bringing together a body of information and ideas that had not been assembled in this form before: where mosque schools existed in Redbridge, their leadership, underlying philosophy, their style of working and curricula, and so on.

As the person who did the drafting, it was, for me, a demanding exercise. It involved, amongst other things, looking very closely at the methods used in mosque schools. It also meant identifying key Muslim/Arabic terms that I had not encountered before, such as *maktab*, *hifz* and *jubba*. In order to ensure accuracy, I met with a local *imam*—a member of the LEA/Mosque Schools working group and representative of a new generation of Muslim imams who had been born in Britain and who had attended not only state schools but also a British Muslim *dar ul-uloom*—and tried, with his assistance, to understand and articulate how mosque schools functioned.

And so, there were two contexts in which I now found myself working—the one, the LEA/mosque schools group, the other my meetings with the imam—each bringing together people from different backgrounds, Muslim and non-Muslim, for a common purpose.

The underlying dynamics of this were compelling. In the case of my work with the imam, for example, we were individuals from different cultural, religious, generational and educational backgrounds but were, nevertheless, working rigorously together to create clarity, insight and understanding. It required time but also trust, patience, openness, and good humour. Moreover, it was obvious that we were both personally and professionally challenged and enriched by the experience. There was also a profound sense that we represented two educational traditions—the one associated with historical Islam, the other with the current British LEA system—and that their engagement with each other could be mutually enriching.

In short, this collaborative work both epitomised and suggested the thrust of this thesis: that contact between the Muslim supplementary educational system and the wider educational community could bring benefits to both sectors.

1.3   The historical roots of the British Muslim community[1]

A Muslim presence within mainland British society can be traced back many centuries (Lewis 2002, p10f; Malik 2004, p64f), with sizeable numbers of Muslims settling in Britain from the end of the eighteenth century (Ansari 2004, pp24–40). It is only relatively recently, however, that it has been possible to conceive of Muslims as comprising a large and significant community within British society. It was the large-scale migrations from the Indian subcontinent and other former British colonies in the decades following the mid-twentieth century that created this strong Muslim presence within Britain.

Though the phrase the 'British Muslim community' is useful as a kind of shorthand and, as such, will be used throughout this book, it must be used with caution, however.[2] For Muslims in Britain, whether at local or national level, have always represented a wide diversity of ethnic, religious, linguistic and social backgrounds:

> Islam in Britain is far from being a monolith; it is a matrix of national, ethnic, doctrinal and economic diversities where variables like age, education, class, ethno-regional background and attitudes towards religion and the non-Muslim communities determine an entire plethora of variegated responses. Indisputably, the basic belief system and practices remain the same, yet sectarian and other such diversities characterise the Muslim diaspora in the United Kingdom. (Malik 2004, p93)[3]

Furthermore, as Ansari (2004, *passim*) makes clear, shifting and constantly renegotiated perceptions of identify have meant that groups and individuals, depending on particular circumstances, have not always regarded themselves first and foremost as 'Muslim' (rather than, for example, as Pakistani, Somali or Arab). Thus:

> [c]aution needs to be exercised in relation to invoking religion as an important feature of Muslim communities in Britain since it concealed a great deal of diversity and interlocked with other, secular, forms of identity. (Ansari 2004, p211)

It seems clear that a significant proportion of first large-scale Muslim immigrants, whether the first family members to arrive or subsequent immigrants who came through the process of 'chain migration'[4] (see eg: Shaw 2000, p22; Ansari 2004, pp148–152), saw their stay in Britain as temporary. They would stay in Britain, establish themselves financially, before returning 'back home' (Bhatti 1999, *passim*) richer and with enhanced status, there 'to retire in dignity and in comfort' (Ansari 2004, p154). This mindset that, after Anwar (1979), is usually referred to as 'the myth of return', gradually faded, however, as Muslim communities grew up in Britain and second and subsequent generation family members came to regard Britain as 'home', rather than the original homeland of their parents and family group.

Though accurate figures are notoriously difficult to determine (Lewis 2002, pp13–16), it is probable that, by the end of the twentieth century, the Muslim community in Britain had grown to about 2,000,000. As such, it is frequently referred to in the media as the largest minority religious group living in Britain. The 2001 census did indeed show that the largest faith group after that of Christians (71%) was that of Muslims (just under 3%). It also showed that nearly 46% of Muslims living in England and Wales were born in the UK and that there are Muslims in every local authority except the Isles of Scilly (Hussain 2004). The census also showed the age imbalance of the British Muslim community with over half of British Muslims being under the age of 25 (Hussain 2004).[5]

1.4 Redbridge and its Muslim community[6]

Redbridge is an Outer London borough, to the north-east of the city. The southern part of the borough, containing the town of Ilford, consists of urban conurbation whilst the northern part contains some large open spaces and wooded areas.

The 2001 national census showed Redbridge as having a population of just under a quarter of a million. This census showed that, proportionately, Redbridge had a far greater diversity of religions than England and Wales as a whole, those nominating themselves as Christian comprising 50.7% of the population. Of non-Christian groups, the Muslim was the largest with 11.9% of the Redbridge population, followed by the Hindu (7.8%), the Jewish (6.2%), the Sikh (5.5%) and the Buddhist (0.4%). Religion also appeared to play a more prominent role in people's lives within Redbridge in that only 9.6% of residents stated that they had 'no religion' compared to a national figure of 15% (London Borough of Redbridge 2005, p6).

No detailed study has been carried out on the Redbridge Muslim population as a whole, or on individual groupings within it. In terms of size, however, one local source (Ilford Islamic Centre 2003, p6), estimates the Muslim population to have been between only 1000 and 1500 in 1971. Thirty years later, by contrast, 2001 census figures showed that 28,487 Redbridge citizens categorised themselves as 'Muslim', thus constituting the twelfth largest Muslim population in England and Wales (Office for National Statistics 2003).[7]

In terms of heritage groupings within the Redbridge Muslim population, it is evident that a significant proportion of Redbridge Muslims come from what the 2001 census categorises as a 'British Asian or Asian: Indian' background (13.96% of total Redbridge population, over double the percentage of London as a whole). Significant numbers of Redbridge Muslims also come from a 'British Asian or Asian: Pakistani' (6.24% of total population) or 'British Asian or Asian: Bangladeshi' (1.17% of total population) background (London Borough of Redbridge 2005, pp2–3). Over recent years, however, there has been a considerable movement of refugees into Redbridge, including those from traditional Muslim homelands such as Somalia. That the Muslim population of Redbridge is predominantly Sunni is attested by the fact that there is no Shi'a centre within its boundaries.[8]

The age distribution of the Redbridge Muslim population mirrors the imbalance in favour of the younger age groups that is found nationally (1.3). Thus, though the 2001 national census showed that about 12% of the total Redbridge population consisted of Muslims (see above), local education authority figures based on parental returns indicated that the proportion of Muslim children in LEA schools was significantly higher: about 21%. By 2005 this had increased to 23% in all borough schools, with a significantly higher figure in primary schools (27%) compared to secondary (19%).

Given the size of the Redbridge Muslim population, it is not surprising that, of the over 950 Muslim associations in Britain (Cesari 2005, p1021), a number of Muslim organisations have originated there. This includes the League of British Muslims, UK, and the Muslim Public Affairs Committee (MPACUK), an organisation that, through skilful use of the Internet, propagates its mission as 'the UK's leading Muslim civil liberties group' (MPACUK website).

At least ten Muslim centres exist in Redbridge in 2006, an increase from the number identified in 2003 (Redbridge SACRE 2003, p3), though only two of them include fully or partly purpose-built mosque buildings. Architecturally speaking, the most spectacular mosque building is that of the Ilford Mosque and Islamic Society which has recently added a large purpose-built two-storey community centre to its estate. The community that uses this mosque is predominantly *Barelvi* by tradition. It was from this group that, in the 1980s, a predominantly *Deobandi*-orientated group, largely of Gujarati heritage, hived off to form its own distinct mosque and associated community: Ilford Muslim Society (6.2). Such divisions within British Islam along what appear to be Deobandi/Barelvi lines have been noted elsewhere (Nielsen 1995, p45) though, if the judgement of Geaves is correct—that it was more common in major British Muslim communities for Barelvi-orientated Muslims to split off from what had become Deobandi-managed mosques (Geaves 1996, pp159–160)—the reverse situation in Ilford would be untypical.

1.5 The growing public interest in emergent British Islam

As has already been noted (1.3), it is only in recent years that it has been possible to conceive of Muslims as constituting a sizeable and significant component of British society.

Consistent with an historical ambivalence towards Muslims—regarded at one and the same time, for instance, as both exotic and rich as well as lascivious and cruel (see, eg, Said 1997, pp3–35)—modern British media have displayed ambivalence towards Islam in general and the British Muslim community in particular. At worst, and particularly in the shadow of '9/11' in the United States and '7/7' in Britain, sensationalist reporting has drawn from the wells of old, stereotypical images of the Muslim: the syndrome of the 'Infidel Within', to use Humayun Ansari's phrase (2004). It is such images that have fed into that disposition that has been dubbed 'Islamophobia', a neologism that probably first appeared in print in February 1991 (The Runnymede Trust 1997, p1 n4).

But alongside such crude, negative and patronising depictions, paralleling more serious academic writing and research by both Muslims and non-Muslims, there is substantial evidence that there is a growing public interest in the nature of the emergent British Muslim community: its internal dynamics and tensions as well as the consequences of its existence as a minority group, albeit a substantial one, within a larger non-Muslim culture.

The scope of this interest, together with the inherent desire to move beyond traditional stereotypes of Islam and the Muslim community, can be demonstrated through a brief review of five BBC radio and television programmes that were broadcast within the eight-month period, July 2004 to March 2005 (see 3.7).

The pan-European backdrop to this more substantial enquiry was evident in the first of the series of programmes, 'Who controls Europe's Muslims?' (BBC Radio 4, 2004a): a concern about the implications of the presence of a sizeable Muslim community (said to be about 14 million) throughout Europe. Noting the key role of the imam within the Muslim community, the programme investigated the attempts by a number of European governments—notably the Dutch, French, and British—to control the importation of imams from traditional Islamic lands and to regulate their adaptation to the European setting. The programme also explored the training and perspectives of what it termed 'a new breed of European imam': that is, European-born Muslims who, through study and training, have attained the status of imams in their own European communities.

An interest in the role of the imam in general, and the imam's place within the emergent British Muslim community with its numerical weighting towards the young (1.3) in particular, was taken up in three of the other programmes.

Each programme, in its own way, explored the tension that exists within contemporary British Islam between the 'traditional' imam—often with poor English language skills and 'imported' from a rural area in a country like Pakistan—and the newer breed of 'home-grown' imams—born or brought up in Britain, native English-speaking, and having a good grasp of contemporary British culture. Each programme also touched on the idea that the latter might have a significant role not only within the emergent British Muslim community but also beyond it.

In 'Rookie Imams' (BBC Radio 4, 2004c), two British institutions for the training of imams were visited: the Muslim College in Ealing (founded by Dr Zaki Badawi in 1989) and a traditional dar ul-uloom in Leicester. It was not difficult to find contrasts between these institutions, but it was the words of two young students from the more traditional dar ul-uloom that suggested a radically more inclusive engagement with British society as a whole:

> Whatever talents we have, we'll endeavour to use these talents in whichever field we can to serve humanity. I live in Britain and Britain has given a lot to me. And I feel the people of Britain deserve something back from me and that's what I intend to do.

This notion of Muslim imams not only serving British Muslims but also having a role in wider society was also taken up in 'Muslim scholars at Eton College' (BBC Radio 4, 2004d). This programme explored the implication of the decision by Eton College to appoint two Muslim teachers, one a trained imam, not only to address the needs of the small number of Muslim pupils at the school but also to contribute to the education and experience of other, non-Muslim students.

In the BBC Two television programme, 'Who wants to be a Mullah?' (BBC Two, 2005), the idea that the British Muslim community is one in transition, with the role of the imam having to be seen in wider, more inclusive terms, was clearly evident in the closing words of the British Pakistani commentator:

> Call them what you want—imams, clerics, or religious leaders—after speaking to them, it was clear that they weren't the mad mullahs portrayed by some sections of the press. The imams I've met in the last few months have made me realise that genuine efforts are being made to connect with the new generation of British Pakistanis ... What's clear to me is that this new breed are role models for their followers and are fast becoming ambassadors of their faith to the wider British society.

That such aspirations must be counterbalanced with other less laudable aspects of the British Muslim community, however, was demonstrated in the radio 'File on 4' programme broadcast in July 2004 (BBC Radio 4, 2004b). This programme focused on the secrecy that exists within many mosque communities so that there are pressures to cover up allegations of both financial mismanagement and physical abuse of children by mosque teachers. The programme suggested that, in the light of some high-profile criminal cases, the traditional Muslim response—that the community itself will deal with matters that arise—is no longer adequate.

1.6 The continuing debate about the efficacy of traditional Islamic education

Given the importance placed on knowledge, learning and education in Islam (2.2), it is not surprising that the educational needs of the British Muslim community were being addressed from the earliest days of British Muslim settlement. This resulted in both literary and academic projects, associated with centres like Woking Mosque (Ansari 2004, pp126–134, 341; Malik 2004, pp83–84) and Muslim entrepreneurs, scholars and activists such as Abdullah Quilliam (c1856–1932) (Mogra 2004, p21)[9] and the Qur'anic translators Marmaduke Pickthall (1875–1936) (Clark 1986) and Abdullah Yusuf Ali (1872–1953) (Sherif 2004). It also led to the setting up of local provision for the religious teaching of young Muslims.

Although local Muslim provision for the teaching of the young has always been, and continues to be, varied in form and style (see ch 4), as soon as Muslim centres of population had been sufficiently established, such provision generally included the holding of classes at the local mosque or mosques. The classes at a particular mosque are often referred to colloquially as a *madrasah*, though some Muslims prefer the term 'maktab' for mosque school provision, reserving the term *madrasah* for more formal institutions—dar ul-uloom—which include higher Islamic studies, often for students well into their twenties.

There is clear evidence, from within the British Muslim community, of dissatisfaction with the quality and form of much mosque-based education (4.7 and below). There have been two major factors, however, that have tended to mask this.

The first has been a desire within Muslim communities to keep evidence of internal dissension or disagreement away from the enquiring gaze of the larger non-Muslim community (1.5). Such a view has often made accusations of child abuse difficult for local government agencies to investigate (BBC Radio 4, 2004b).

The second has been the tendency in much literature to focus on Muslim schooling almost exclusively in terms of independent or voluntary-aided institutions at the expense of mosque supplementary classes. In his extensive chapter on 'British Muslims and Education', for example, Ansari makes only one or two passing, undeveloped references to 'supplementary' schooling within the Muslim community (Ansari 2004, pp298–339).

Criticism of mosque-based education does exist, however, and has focused on a number of inter-related issues. A number of these issues have revolved around the relationship between imams, people whose traditional role in the mosque has involved teaching, and the children being taught. Historically, the majority of such imams have been trained overseas and then brought in by Muslim communities to serve in their mosques (1.5). Because the majority of British Muslims have a South Asian ancestry, a large number of such imams have been brought in from rural, Urdu- or Mirpuri-speaking areas of Pakistan. As the British community developed and second and third generation British Muslim children began to attend mosque classes, an obvious disjuncture became apparent: Pakistani-trained imams, often with little or no English, teaching young, British Muslims:

> Given their lack of familiarity with the British urban environment and understanding of it, these religious leaders—usually village *imams*—were unable to provide appropriate guidance and inevitably responded by using these institutions to preserve religio-cultural practices from another world. (Ansari 2004, p344)

> They may be knowledgeable people but they do not know the Western society very well so they do not know the knowledge base and the nature of the pupils that they're teaching so there's not much good relationship between the teacher and his pupils. There's some sort of gap. (Interview with Muslim scholar, Cambridge, January 2003)

One form of criticism, then, has been that these imams neither understand the world nor the concerns of children growing up as British Muslims. 'The imams', said an adult Muslim speaking of his childhood in Britain, 'didn't seem to know much about the world I was living in' (BBC Two 2005).

Associated with this mismatch of worlds (and worldviews) have been reports that some imams and mosque teachers have been harsh disciplinarians. This has included the use of corporal punishment which, though perhaps conventional in a more traditional rural environment (2.3), is both out of context and illegal within the British setting. Interviewed in a BBC Radio 4 programme, for instance, a Muslim man reported that his brother:

> was near enough in tears. He was saying that he was reading and he made a mistake and the teacher hit him, slapped him in the face, hit him on the head and also swore at him. (BBC Radio 4, 2004b)

In his research into the perspectives of 9–11 year-olds in three inner-city multi-ethnic schools, Greg Smith recorded that:

> children frequently talked about the strict discipline they encountered at mosque ... Many discussed with us the fact that punishment in some, but by no means all, mosques involved children being hit with a stick on

the back or hands, or being made to stand or squat in uncomfortable positions for long periods. (Smith 2005, p56)

As has already been implied, such methods were an importation from other cultures and conditions; in his biography of his Indian-born father, Hanif Kureishi recalls that 'Father had talked about the childhood monotony of having to learn the Koran (*sic*) by rote, and of being hit with sticks by the Moulvis [*malvis*]'. (Kureishi 2004, p203) Fieldwork evidence (chapter 4) suggests that one of the reasons why some Muslim children have left mosque school to be educated at home by family or a tutor is because of their disturbing experiences at the hands of imams in the mosque school setting.

Further criticisms have focused on the style of learning that takes place in mosque schools, notably the elements of rote-learning and memorisation. Not only, it has been said, do such methods fail to engage the interest of youngsters, whose 'experiences of rote learning without any understanding left them bored and alienated not only from the madrasa (*sic*) but from religion itself' (*Q News*, October/November 2000: cited in Lewis 2002, p221) but also such learning styles inhibit students and do not equip them for life in contemporary British society. Mohammad Raza was of this view when, writing in 1991, he said:

> The plain fact of the matter is that nothing should be taught to children that they cannot understand. If children or young adults cannot understand what they have memorized, how can they defend themselves when their beliefs are attacked by non-believers? (Raza 1991, p59)

Almost fifteen years later, a Pakistani Muslim, speaking of his British childhood, recollected that:

> [a]s a young boy, those I came across barely spoke English. I learned to read the Qur'an without ever understanding a word of it. In my teens, the Urdu sermons coupled with the Arabic flew right over my head. (BBC Two, 2005)

Another criticism of the learning that takes place in mosque classes has focused on the amount of time that young Muslims spend there each day after their time at 'day' school. This is not only a concern voiced frequently by non-Muslim mainstream teachers, but has also been voiced within the Muslim community:

> [T]he student, after spending a good part of the day at school, comes exhausted both mentally and physically to the *madrasa* [*sic*]. If the [teacher] then conducts his lessons without any preparation, planning or using relevant methods, how would that then capture the imagination, attention and hearts of the students? (Institute of Islamic Scholars, Batley, Yorkshire, first bi-annual report, 2000–2 quoted in Lewis 2004, p178)

1.7 The increasing use of networking within the educational community

Within British education, the last decades of the twentieth century and the first decade of the twenty-first have seen a growing interest in how best learning might be promoted and fostered. This has spawned a lively growth industry in which individuals have developed and promoted particular learning-enhancing techniques, such as 'mind-mapping' (eg Buzan 2000) and 'accelerated learning' (eg Smith 1998). Since its official launch in November 2000, the National College for School Leadership[10] (NCSL) took a national lead in research and development into school leadership issues. This included a wide range of projects associated with 'networking', a loose concept that refers to individuals or organisations working together, at different levels, in order to share experience, carry out projects, refine practice and generate new knowledge and understanding.

Networks in general have been described as 'the language of our times' (McCarthy et al 2004, p11) and heralded as the 'most important organisational form' in the world today (Hannon 2005), and, coupled with collaboration, regarded as one of the four 'key drivers to raise achievement and build capacity for the next stage of reform' (Hopkins 2005). The formal use and exploration of educational networks, however, can be traced back to the USA during the last three decades of the twentieth century (Lieberman 1999). Some of the educational networks that have operated in the USA—those associated with the 'Annenberg Challenge' reform initiative in Los Angeles, for example—have been researched in order to identify overall effectiveness and causal factors, including their implicit redistribution of power (Wohlstetter et al 2003).

In the United Kingdom, a major initiative associated with NCSL, a key objective of which was to 'promote collaborative learning and communication', was to set up so-called 'networked learning communities' involving more than 1,000 schools across England. The project involved 'groups of schools working together in partnership with other educational bodies such as LEAs, universities and community partners for the benefit of one another and the whole educational system'. (NCSL)

NCSL both encouraged debate about the role of networks (eg Desforges 2005, Jackson 2005) and developed a detailed and elaborate rationale to underpin this work. Networked learning communities, for example, were supposed to engage in six 'levels' of learning, that is: pupil learning, staff learning, leadership learning, within school learning, school to school learning, and network to network learning. The associated literature also referred to three 'fields of knowledge': what we know, what is known, and new knowledge. Various collaborative investigative techniques, such as 'learning walks'—in which groups of staff visited other settings in order to consider various themes—and 'research lessons', in which teachers jointly planned a lesson, observed the teaching of it and considered its value—were also advocated.

This style of initiating, propagating and sharing good practice was adopted by the Department of Education and Skills (DfES)[11] as part of its National Primary Strategy, the formal means of putting into practice those principles and proposals set out in its document *Excellence and Enjoyment* (DfES 2003), in collaboration with NCSL. The associated literature listed a variety of benefits that school-to-school networking could bring, including creating 'new opportunities for adult learning' (DfES/NCSL 2005). Though some have detected an uncritical stance towards networks (eg Hargreaves in McCarthy et al 2004), the *zeitgeist* of educational networking is that collaborative effort, within a decentralised context, in which 'school improvement is driven from within' (Jackson 2005), accomplishes more than individual effort. But, more than this, if the right structure and spirit are generated, it can produce a wide range of valuable outcomes, including 'opportunities for teachers to both consume and generate knowledge', 'discussion of problems that often have no agreed-upon solutions', and 'a vision of reform that excites and encourages risk taking in a supportive environment' (Lieberman 1999).

1.8 The growing official recognition of the contribution made by supplementary schooling

Running parallel to this increasing involvement of schools and other educational institutions in networking programmes was a drive, both nationally and locally, to create conditions in which people and groups from a wide range of backgrounds, including religious and cultural, could work together for the common good.

Such a drive was evident in much official documentation such as *Every Child Matters: Working with voluntary community organisations to deliver change for children and young people* (DfES 2004) which advocated voluntary and official organisations 'working together at local level' (p29). That community-based supplementary schools had a role to play in this situation of local regeneration was made clear in the document *Aiming High* (DfES 2003):

> Many pupils have ... benefited greatly from out-of-school hours learning in community-run initiatives such as supplementary schools ... Attendance can enhance pupils' self-respect, promote self-discipline and inspire pupils to have high aspirations to succeed. (DfES 2003, 2.36)

This growing official recognition of the contribution made by supplementary schooling was actualised in a number of organisations.

At national level, the DfES-funded Supplementary Schools Support Service ('S4') was officially launched in January 2001 in order to offer support to the wide range of supplementary schools then in existence. This service, which operated until 2004, was succeeded by the website-based 'Supplementary Schools Network' that was established by the 'stakeholders' themselves (Supplementary Schools Network website).[12]

Whether because of an increasing technological capacity to network, the political drive to bring different groups together to work for mutual benefit, or particular local circumstances, a number of local education authorities (LEAs) also established organisations to support, enhance and develop the work carried out by supplementary schools. Whereas such projects might be limited in scope—the Kirklees 'Madressahs (*sic*) and Supplementary Schools Project', for example, was established specifically to serve the Muslim community through promoting 'a good understanding of child protection issues' and developing 'appropriate policies and procedures' (Madressahs and Supplementary Schools Project website)—others were broader in both intention and client grouping. One of the aims of the 'Birmingham Supplementary Schools Forum', for instance, was to:

> [p]romote the value of Supplementary Schools and establish linkages with Mainstream Schools particularly through out-of-hours school activities and sharing good practice.

Furthermore, one of its 'key strands of development' was the 'Development of linkages to Mainstream School' (Birmingham Supplementary Schools Forum website).

In terms of the scope of this study, the 'Leicester Complementary Schools Trust' was particularly interesting in so far as it emerged out of a joint University of Leicester/University of Birmingham research project funded by the Economic and Social Research Council. The project was divided into two phases: the first consisting of a survey of supplementary schools in Leicester, the second an ethnographic case study of two supplementary schools. A report on each phase of the project was published (Martin et al 2003, 2004).

Basic to the Leicester project was the notion that supplementary schools were to be seen as making a positive contribution to the wider educational scene: thus the choice of the title *'complementary* schools':

> Defining these particular schools as *complementary schools* stresses the positive complementary factor for those who teach or learn in them. It recognizes the importance for participants and their local black and ethnic minority communities and their potential contribution to political, social and economic life in the wider community. (Martin et al 2004, p7)

One of the main findings of this project was 'the vivid way in which complementary schools add value and enhance learning across other settings'. As such, the researchers wrote: 'There are many telling examples in our data set that illustrate how practices in the school can enhance learning in other contexts' (Martin et al 2004, p14).

It is appropriate, then, that one of the aims of the Leicester Complementary Schools Trust was to 'enhance and develop the relationship with mainstream schools utilising principles of collaborative advantage to improve the quality of teaching and learning' (Martin et al 2004, p18).

The eight sections of this chapter have sought not only to set a broad context for this study but also to bring together evidence in support of its timeliness. Building on this foundation, the next chapter will review the range of literature that was consulted. In doing so, it will also set the research within the context of Muslim beliefs about, and attitudes towards, knowledge, learning and education.

2 Literature Review

2.1 Introduction

As well as reviewing the wide range and types of literature that were consulted during the course of research, this chapter has two further aims: first, to provide further contextual material to underpin the fieldwork that is at the heart of this study (chapters 4, 5 and 6); second, to indicate how this thesis both builds on and extends previous research in this field.

Although a core of academic works and writings was consulted, the genres of material used were wider than this. These included school manuals (2.2), autobiographies (2.3, 2.4), novels (2.3, 2.4), Muslim periodicals (2.4), information gleaned through interviewing Muslims (2.4), and material available on the Internet (see 2.7).

The literature that is reviewed in this chapter concerns the major focus of this study: that is, knowledge, learning and education in Islam. Following a brief survey of the significance of these three elements within Islam (2.2), there is reference to literature and ideas concerning: the culture of traditional Islamic education and learning (2.3); hearing, learning and reciting the Qur'an (2.4); British Islam (2.5); and Muslim educational life in Britain (2.6). The chapter ends with a brief note on the role of cyber information.

In order to maintain clarity and coherence, it was decided to place four other reviews of literature at those places in this study where they most logically belong. Thus, chapter 1 includes a review of literature relating to educational networking (1.7) and chapter 3 to methodological literature concerning ethnography, oral history and life-story research (3.2, 3.3). Chapter 7 includes a review of literature relating to the use of the 'capital' metaphor across a range of academic disciplines (7.2) as well as to memory and memorisation (7.5).

2.2   Knowledge, learning and education in Islam[13]

Whereas there is little available ethnographic material on the life and work of Muslim supplementary classes (2.6), there is a potentially overwhelming body of material relating to knowledge, learning and education in Islam. Some of this latter material was consulted in order to gain a necessary understanding, but care had to be taken so as not to create an imbalance between this and the main focus of the study.

The different translations of surah 96 of the Qur'an, by tradition believed to be the first words to have been revealed to the Prophet Muhammad, indicate the theological and epistemological base of Islam: that the Divine (Allah) desires to impart knowledge to human beings so that they might learn, understand, and follow the right path. Though Yusuf Ali's translation of the Qur'an into English (1983) is often quoted, the fresh translation by Michael Sells in his *Approaching the Qur'an: The Early Revelations* (1999)—together with the transliteration and recorded recitation that he provides—is very accessible:

1. Recite in the name of your Lord who created –
2. From an embryo created the human
3. Recite your lord is all-giving
4. Who taught by the pen

5. Taught the human what he did not know before.

(Sells 1999, p96)

Helen Boyle's *Quranic* [sic] *Schools: Agents of Preservation and Change* (2004) was useful primarily for its material on mosque schools in a number of non-European cultures (2.4), but she also provides some incidental information on the epistemological dimension of the Qur'an: that within the Qur'an, for instance, the word *'ilm* (knowledge—note its root link with the word *uloom*) appears 750 times, ranking it as the third most used term after *Allah* and *Rabb* (Lord)[14] (Boyle 2004, p14).[15]

A substantial amount of the *hadith* literature in Islam also throws light on Muslim approaches to knowledge, learning and education. In one article alone, for example—and that on 'Societal Problems and Education in Pakistan' (Ghaffar 2001)—the following four separate hadith are cited:

'(To) seek knowledge from the cradle to the grave, and acquire it even though it be in China.'

'He dies not who seeks knowledge. Whoever reveres the learned reveres me.'

'To seek knowledge is the duty of every Muslim man and Muslim woman.'

'An hour's contemplation and study of God's creation is better than a year of adoration.'

These four separate hadith were used by Al-Ghazali in his famous 'Book of Knowledge' (*Kitab al-'ilm*) (Ghaffar 2001, p66). And it is in Al-Ghazali (1058–1111 CE) that we find personified the Muslim ideal: a life of knowledge-seeking combined with great personal piety. In his *The Faith and Practice of Al-Ghazali* (Watt 1994), Montgomery Watt demonstrates this in his translation of two of Al-Ghazali's key works,

Deliverance from Error and *The Beginnings of Guidance*. Take, for example, the following statements of Al-Ghazali: 'Really useful knowledge is that which makes you grow in the fear of God' (Watt 1994, p119) and 'ignorance is better for you than all knowledge which does not draw you away from the world toward the next' (Watt 1994, p141). It is a *sine qua non* of the teacher, then, that personal life and bearing must match up to that which is being taught. As such, Al-Ghazali is condemnatory of the scholar/teacher 'if he turns men from this world by what he says, yet he calls them to it by what he is and what he does' (Watt 1994, p110).[16]

Given the centrality of knowledge and learning within the Muslim worldview, and the way in which Muhammad is regarded as the model of the Muslim life, it is not surprising that he has had an influence on Muslim approaches to education in general and to pedagogy in particular (such as repeating things three times: see, for example, Al-Sadan 1999, pp16–17; Abu Ghuddah 2003, pp36–37).[17] Indeed, it has been said of Muhammad not only that '[t]his teacher and this great tutor—there is no human who is a greater teacher than him' (2003, p8) but also that:

> [h]is tradition is considered the source of all Islamic education. As he is the archetype of all necessary learning for Muslims, an awareness of his skills may improve educational performance. (Al-Sadan 1999, p5)

If this is so, then a possible dilemma arises which is of relevance to this study: if Muhammad is the model not only of the rightly-guided human being but also of the Muslim teacher, is there room for moving beyond the range of methods that he employed? Can modern insights and technology be used in order to better the quality of Muslim education? In his 'The pedagogy of the Prophet' (1999), Al-Sadan's response combines adroitly both pedagogical and faith elements in a way that demonstrates the normative status of knowledge and truth in Islam:

> We of the 20th century can respect his methods but could not improve on their moral content. It might, however, be possible to find teaching methods which faithfully respect his manner and his message, but also

reflect the character of communication in our present age. (Al-Sadan 1999, p17)

In his writings on Islamic education, Mark Halstead adopts an apologetic stance similar to that used in this study: that the basis of Islamic education must be understood in order to articulate its key features and draw out its relationship to contemporary Western paradigms of education. Thus, in his 'Towards a Unified View of Islamic Education', Halstead says of the Muslim approach to education:

> Education is ... not to be seen as an end in itself, but as a way of bringing children more into line with God's purposes. Faith in God is axiomatic and is a major factor in determining who is to do the teaching, how and where the teaching is to be carried out and what is to be taught. (Halstead 1995, p31)

Halstead is also one of a number of commentators (eg Boyle 2004, p15) who points to the holistic nature of Muslim education; that it seeks to develop, in harmony with each other, *tarbiya* (individual development),[18] *ta'dib* (social development) and *ta'lim* (transmission of knowledge) (Halstead 1995, p27f).[19]

But what of the role of reason, particularly that exercised by the individual, that is so valued within contemporary Western non-Muslim culture and education? Halstead points out that, though reason is valued within the Muslim world-view, it is not absolute for it must defer to that higher knowledge that has come to humankind through divine revelation:

> any pursuit of knowledge may be viewed as a form of worship in Islam so long as it is undertaken within the boundaries defined by revelation. The educational consequences of this are clear: whatever other knowledge is to be transmitted through education, the knowledge which is derived from divine revelation is obligatory. (Halstead 1995, p30)

Like Boyle (2004), Halstead is also significant in trying to present a reasonable, unjaundiced view of Muslim education. In discussing why modern Islamic educationalists still find much that is of value in traditional Muslim education, for example, he states that:

> [t]here is a natural integration of the curriculum, there is a close personal relationship between the teacher and the taught, élitism is discouraged, undue attention is not paid to examinations, pupil grouping is less rigid and students are comparatively free to pursue their own interests. Above all, traditional Muslim education is not an activity separated from other aspects of society; it is rooted in the community it serves, responding to its needs and aspirations and preserving its values and beliefs. (Halstead 1995, p32)

But, in contrast to what will later be developed in this study (chapters 7 and 8), Halstead demonstrates little apparent sympathy for traditional Muslim educational practices like memorisation. Indeed, he quotes the great Muslim educationalist and philosopher Ibn Khaldun (1332–1382 CE) who defined education as 'a special skill whose aim is to establish the faculty of knowledge in those who learn, rather than to force them to memorise the offshoots of knowledge' (Halstead 1995, p32).

2.3   The culture of traditional Islamic education and learning

If the Muslim stance towards knowledge, learning and education can be delineated (2.2), how does this translate into historical practice, particularly in different Muslim cultural settings?

Francis Robinson's chapter on 'Knowledge, its Transmission and the Making of Muslim Societies' (Robinson 1999) provides an accessible means of grasping the historic development of Islamic education. Robinson, for example, outlines the impact of modern technology, including the 'democratisation' of knowledge that it has brought, on the traditional role of Muslim scholars, the *ulama* (Robinson 1996, pp246–249). He also traces the origins of the madrasah as the centre *par excellence* of Islamic learning (see also Mortel 1996)[20] and notes the characteristics of traditional Islamic learning: informality and oral transmission between student and teacher:

> Muslims were fundamentally sceptical of the written word, and particularly the written word studied without supervision, as a reliable means of communication. (Robinson 1996, p223)

There is, however, little available material which gives an understanding of what the process of going through a traditional pattern of Islamic education actually 'felt' or 'feels' like for people: how it affects their daily routines, relationships, thought-patterns and expectations of life.[21]

It is in providing this that Dale F Eickelman's *Knowledge and Power in Morocco: The Education of a Twentieth-Century Notable* (1985) is of inestimable value (see also Eickelman 1978). As well as being an ethnographic *tour de force* (see Clifford Geertz's foreword: Eickelman 1985, ppxi–xiv), this 'social biography' portrays the status of knowledge, learning and education within an actual social setting—twentieth century Morocco—and in the life of an individual—the Moroccan *qadi* (judge), 'Abd ar-Rahman Mansuri (b. 1912).

Eickelman makes it clear that, though there are common principles underlying Muslim approaches to learning and education, emphases will vary between different cultures. Dominant within the Moroccan was an emphasis on what he terms 'mnemonic possession': that is, 'the basic popular and learned paradigm of valued knowledge as fixed and memorizable' (Eickelman 1985, p164).

He also comments that, 'Even Ibn Khaldun (d. 1406) noted that the role of memory was stressed more in Morocco than elsewhere in the Islamic Middle East' (Eickelman 1985, p58). Having said this, however, Eickelman also notes 'the openness and flexibility of the world of traditional Islamic learning, attributes not generally accorded to it by those who observe it from a distance' (Eickelman 1985, p19: see also p33, pp34–35).

In tracing the acquisition of knowledge, learning and social status during the life of 'Abd ar-Rahman Mansuri, many of the themes that are explored elsewhere in this study are touched upon. Take, for example, the young child's memorisation of the Qur'an at the hands of his father and other teachers, because 'In Moroccan towns and villages, the discipline of Qur'anic memorisation' was 'an integral part of learning to be human and Muslim' (Eickelman 1985, p63). Furthermore, this process involved physical punishment:

> When a father handed his son over to a fqih [Qur'anic teacher], he did so with the formulaic phrase that the child could be beaten as the fqih saw fit. Such punishments were considered necessary for accurate Quranic recitation of the word of God ... Moreover ... students were told that any part of their bodies struck in the process of Quranic recitation would not burn in hell. (Eickelman 1985, p63)

Two of the other traditional features that Eickelman touches on and—because of the nature of his 'social biography', contextualises—relate to an explicit and an implicit characteristic of traditional Muslim education and learning.

The first characteristic is the physical positioning of students in relation to their teacher: the *halaqa* or 'learning circle', a practice said to date from the Prophet Muhammad himself (Council on Islamic Education, p82; Boyle 2004, p11). The second characteristic derives from the normative view of knowledge that we have already noted (2.2) as well as the high regard that teachers, as authoritative transmitters of knowledge, are held within the Islamic world:

> No questions were asked during these [teaching] sessions, and students rarely took notes or made annotations in the printed copies of texts that a few possessed. Former students explained that deference and propriety towards their shayks prevented their openly raising any issues ... Questions had to be placed indirectly ... so as not to suggest a public challenge to his scholarship. (Eickelman 1985, p95)

Historically, such traditional approaches to Islamic education were to become challenged increasingly by other paradigms of knowledge, learning and education. In general, such paradigms were presented through the rise of modernism and the increasing material and intellectual dominance of the technologically rich West. In particular, however, national Muslim communities often faced this challenge through the process of being colonised. Indeed, Eickelman himself notes that this was already happening in French-colonised Morocco (Eickelman 1985, p8).

Only one novel has been located which provides an imaginative, insider account of traditional Islamic education (with its attendant worldview) and what happens when this is challenged by other world-views and educational systems: *Ambiguous Adventure* by Cheikh Hamidou Kane (1972). The Muslim Senegalese world that this novel portrays resonates both with Eickelman's Morocco and with aspects of the culture of the North London mosque school in which the fieldwork for this study took place.

Here, again, we find the use of the 'learning circle' (pp22, 65) and, from the very first page, the use of physical means to encourage concentration and accurate pronunciation. But we also find other aspects of traditional Muslim learning. There is, for example, the reverence with which the 'incandescent text' (Kane 1972, pp4–5) of the Qur'an is treated and the practice of learning the text before its meaning. Indeed, part of the tragedy of Samba Diallo, the key character in the unfolding story, in leaving his Qur'anic learning in order to attend a French colonial school is that it broke the transition from the former to the latter. Thus, later in life, he grieves on leaving his teacher before 'he was about to initiate me at last into the rational understanding of what up to then I had done no more than recite—with wonder, to be sure' (Kane 1972, p160). There is also reference to various traditions associated with Qur'anic learning, such as the recitation of the whole Qur'an by a son returning home to his parents (Kane 1972, pp71–73).

But the most powerful element of this novel is its vivid portrayal of the dilemma faced by Muslims when two forms of educational provision—traditional Muslim learning and that provided by the colonial 'foreign schools'—were seen to be in competition with each other, with power and social prestige belonging to the latter. Thus:

> [t]he question is disturbing ... We reject the foreign school in order to remain ourselves, and to preserve for God the place He holds in our hearts. But have we still enough force to resist the school, and enough substance to remain ourselves? (Kane 1972, p10)

The impact at a personal level is evident in the words of Samba Diallo towards the end of the novel. The journey from traditional Qur'anic school to a foreign school and then to a French university has not simply been a journey through different forms of educational provision. Rather, it has affected his relationship with the world and his interpretation of reality:

> Progressively, they brought me out from the heart of things, and accustomed me to live at a distance from the world. (Kane 1972, p160)

2.4   Hearing, learning and reciting the Qur'an[22]

Particularly in relation to chapter 6, it is essential to understand how Muslims engage with the Qur'an as an experience consisting of both word and sound. Though an enormous literature on the Qur'an exists, this consists largely of material such as translations into English, analyses of content, and histories. Much less is available in English on the processes through which, and the social contexts in which, the Qur'an is learned, assimilated, experienced and recited. This derives undoubtedly from the limited understanding within the main body of traditional Western scholarship of the profound role of the Qur'an, as both physical object and sound, within the daily life of Muslim communities both today and in the past.

A number of reasons to account for this lack of understanding have been put forward, including: a negative Christian attitude towards the Qur'an which was believed to have originated in the mind of Muhammad and the milieu in which he lived (Cantwell Smith 1980, p495); the tendency to think of the Qur'an in 'scriptural' and historical terms rather than as a living, dynamic presence within society and within people's lives (Cantwell Smith 1971, 1980; Graham 1985); the nature of Western culture with its bias towards the visual and the textual at the expense of the aural and oral (Ruthven 1984, p80; Graham 1985, p27);[23] the ease of access to Islamic literature in the absence of an Islamic presence in daily life (Nelson 2001, pxviii); and, within the field of world religions, the classification of the Qur'an as part of the genus 'scripture' with its textual connotation (Graham 1985, p27).

It is in providing a corrective to such Western, non-Muslim perceptions of the Qur'an that Kristina Nelson's *The Art of Reciting the Qur'an* (2001) is of such value. But the overarching significance of Nelson's work in the context of this study is in demonstrating that, within the Muslim tradition, the Qur'an is less a text than an oral and aural experience:

> The transmission of the Qur'an and its social existence are essentially oral. Qur'anic rhythm and assonance alone confirm that it is meant to be heard. But the oral nature of the Qur'an goes beyond euphony: the significance of the revelation is carried as much by the sound as by its semantic information. In other words, the Qur'an is not the Qur'an unless it is heard. The familiar sound of recitation is the Muslim's predominant and most immediate means of contact with the word of God. (Nelson 2001, pxiv)

This perception is rooted in the key Muslim belief that the message of God was revealed *in both* sound *and* word to the Prophet Muhammad; in some manner, he *heard* the words. Thus, Muhammad did not pass on inscribed tablets to his fellows but, rather, repeated—sounded out, that is—the divine words that he himself had heard. His companions, in turn, learned these sounded words and passed them on in sound—through recitation—to others.²⁴ Thus:

> [t]he written word does not exist to preserve against change: it is taken for granted that oral tradition does that ... Muhammad spread the message by sending out reciters, not text. (Nelson 2001, p3)

As such, both the experience of learning the sounds of God's words and the act of orally transmitting them to others are part of the bedrock of Muslim tradition.²⁵ This has two profound consequences for Muslim learning and sensibility.

First, it explains why the transmission of the Qur'an remains essentially a personal speaking-and-listening encounter between teacher and student.²⁶ For, the student not only learns the words of the Arabic and commits them to memory, but also learns how these words are to be sounded: 'Learning the Qur'an means learning the correct sound of the Qur'an' (Nelson 2001, p15).²⁷ And, for this, students need to hear recitation from someone who is a faithful transmitter and who must, then, hear the students themselves recite in order to correct them. In turn, the student *qua* teacher will be able to recite in the hearing of future generations of Muslim students. It is no surprise, then, that the Arabic word *hifd* ('memorisation', a cognate term to *hafiz*) also means 'to preserve' (Nelson 2001, p55).

Second, the Muslim belief in the divine source of the Qur'an explains why Muslims approach the sound of its recitation with such reverence and heightened expectation:²⁸

> Ultimately, scholars and listeners recognise that the ideal beauty and inimitability of the Qur'an lie not in the content and order of the message, on the one hand, and in the elegance of the language, on the other, but in the use of the very sound of the language to convey specific meaning. This amounts to an almost onomatopoeic use of language, so that not only the image of the metaphor but also the sound of the words which

express that image are perceived to converge with the meaning. (Nelson 2001, p13)[29]

As with Nelson's work, Sell's *Approaching the Qur'an: The Early Revelations* (1999) does much to present the aural dynamic of the Qur'an to non-Muslim readers. Sells uses the concept of 'sound vision' to articulate the distinctive manner in which the Qur'an intertwines both sound and meaning (Sells 1999, p16 *& passim*) and in which 'the Qur'an shapes sounds in particularly powerful combinations with meaning and feeling to create an effect in which sound and meaning are intertwined' (Sells 1999, p3). As such, he notes the capacity of the sound of Qur'anic recitation to affect Muslims profoundly at an inner level:

> The sound of Qur'anic recitation can move people to tears, from 'Umar, the powerful second Caliph of Islam, to the average farmer, villager, or townspeople of today, including those who may not be particularly observant or religious in temperament. (Sells 1999, p3)

Karen Armstrong—a contemporary Western non-Muslim academic who, in her writings about Islam (Armstrong 1991, 2001), displays great sensitivity to Muslim history, traditions and world-view—provides evidence for this in an incidental reference in her autobiographical *The Spiral Staircase* (2004). The scene is a car journey in East Jerusalem, with four Muslim men (two drinking bottled beer), in 1983. The car radio was broadcasting tinny Arabic music:

> Suddenly the music stopped, there was an announcement, and the atmosphere in the car became very still. 'It's the Qur'an,' Ahmed told me, but with eager anticipation, as though he were expecting a great treat. I was surprised. I knew that Ahmed was not a practising Muslim; in fact, he seemed to dislike religion. Had I been driving in London with beer-drinking secularists and found that we were about to be treated to a reading from the Bible on the radio, somebody would have lunged immediately for the 'off' button. But it was very different here. I listened to the chanted recitation as it filled the car. Periodically one of the men

would make an involuntary exclamation of delight, and soon, feeling sorry for me, they tried to include me in the experience, by translating the text into English, the words tumbling over one another as they tried to express its complexity.[30] (Armstrong 2004, pp279–280)

It is in further understanding the nature of orality and its implications for perception and thought process that Walter J Ong's *Orality and Literacy: The Technologizing of the Word* (1982), is significant. As Ong makes clear, 'the relentless dominance of textuality' (p10) means that it is difficult for those brought up in literate societies to understand the nature of thought processes in societies where there is no recorded text or where oral tradition still has a significant role. The detailed and scholarly approach of Ong is helpfully counterbalanced by Chinua Achebe's novel *No Longer at Ease* (Achebe 1963). Drawing directly on the Ibo oral tradition of West Africa, this portrays the mental and social processes of people living in a culture which is still largely residually oral.

However, though an understanding of the move from 'orality' to 'literacy' is helpful in understanding the nature of human culture, thought-processes and the social power accruing from guardianship of knowledge (Robinson 1996, p246f), there is a danger that this could lead to a reductionist interpretation of Qur'anic recitation: that Qur'anic recitation and memorisation are an anachronistic 'relic' of pre- or proto-literate societies which will change as Muslim societies become more literate. There are elements of such a reductionist position, for example, in Philip Lewis' analysis of 'Between Orality and Literacy: The Dilemma for the Muslim Educator' (Lewis 2002, pp77–81).

Rather, given Muslim beliefs about the nature of the Qur'anic revelation and subsequent transmission, the process of Qur'anic memorisation and recitation remains a necessary element of Muslim education and learning. Furthermore, the nature of religious practice also requires both memorisation and recitation on the part of all Muslims. Learning key *surahs* and passages from the Qur'an, notably those that will be recited during daily *salah* (ritual prayer), forms part of the general nurture and education of Muslim children, whether at the hands of their parents or in a mosque class (chapter 4). Though the rote learning that is used to commit such passages to memory is frequently criticised, the ideal is that the process of memorising is more than a 'mere' mnemonic exercise. For:

> [a]s the students learn these Surahs, they are not simply learning something by rote, but rather interiorising the inner rhythms, sound patterns, and textual dynamics—taking it to heart in the deepest manner. (Sells 1999, p11)

Boyle (2004) develops the concept of 'embodiment' to express the same insight but extends it through suggesting that this will provide an inner resource to be drawn upon incrementally through a person's whole life:

> Qur'anic memorization ... is an educational process whereby the Qur'an becomes embodied within the person of the memorizer, usually a child. Memorization, in this case, is a process that seamlessly unites the physical and the mental in the formation and enactment of religious and cultural practice. Seen in this light, memorization is more than the following of tradition, more than sustained discipline or indoctrination, and even more than the passing on of religious rituals. The embodied Qur'an serves as a source of ongoing knowledge and protection to the child as he/she journeys through life. (Boyle 2004, p83)[31]

In some cases a person might make the decision to commit the whole Qur'an to memory and, within the Sunni tradition of Islam, the person who has achieved this—a *hafiz* (male) or *hafiza* (female)—is an honoured and highly regarded member of society. *Huffaz* have a prominent role in such events as the recitations that take place during *tarawih* prayers across the month of Ramadan (5.2).

In the course of preparing this study, no other English-language research material was identified concerning the process through which a person becomes a hafiz: how and when text is committed to memory, why an individual would want to take this arduous path, and its personal and social consequences.[32] As such, this study—particularly the fieldwork material in chapter 6—makes a significant contribution to research in this field.

2.5 British Islam

There is a substantial and growing literature on British Islam.[33] Much of this demonstrates both the complexity and diversity of the British Muslim scene.

Of the detailed histories, Philip Lewis' *Islamic Britain: Religion, Politics and Identity among British Muslims* (2002) provided a comprehensive overview in the early stages of carrying out this study. In his detailed analysis of the dynamics of the Muslim community in Bradford ('Britain's Islamabad', pp49–75) and exploration of the political, religious and cultural heritage of those many Muslims who came from a South Asian background, Lewis makes clear both the complexity and diversity of 'British Islam'.

Humayun Ansari's *The Infidel Within: Muslims in Britain Since 1800* (2004) complements and develops Lewis in two significant ways. Firstly, he demonstrates how the experience of different groups of Muslim immigrants—those from Bangladeshi, Pakistani, Indian, Turkish Cypriot and Arab backgrounds, for instance—could be markedly different, including socially and economically. Secondly, as we have already noted (1.3), Ansari demonstrates how 'Muslim' can be one of a series of terms that are used in conditions where sense of identity is multi-faceted, complex and shifting.

Many of the groups and sects, the origins and ideologies of which both Lewis and Ansari describe—such as Deobandis, Barelvis and *Tabligh-i Jamaat*—provide the context in which many British Muslims not only define their Muslim identity but also their particular approaches to tradition, knowledge and educational activity. Ron Geaves' *Sectarian*

Influences within Islam in Britain (1996) provides further detail about specific Muslim traditions, Deobandi and Barelvi included, found in Britain. In the context of this study, his treatment of the former is particularly significant in that the fieldwork outlined below in chapters 5 and 6 took place within a predominantly Deobandi-orientated mosque community. In outlining Deobandi origins in India as a group that sought non-participation with governmental and colonial powers, Geaves suggests that this isolationist position was transferred to Britain:

> Despite the claims of Muslim leaders in Britain that Islam is flexible and able to accommodate modern technological society, the *Deobandis* are still utilising the strategy of withdrawal that they used so successfully in British India in order to protect Islam from the threat of secularisation in modern Britain. (Geaves 1996, p167)

The Deobandi 'stance of isolation from the wider British community' (Geaves 1996, p171), yet willingness to engage in the fieldwork that undergirds this study, might be evidence of a shift in position towards one of greater engagement with society at large (Lewis 2004).

A number of works include British Islam within a broader survey. These include Jørgen Nielsen's, *Muslims in Western Europe* (1995), Iftikhar Malik's *Islam and Modernity: Muslims in Europe and the United States* (2004) and, at a less academic and more journalistic level, Adam LeBor's *A Heart Turned East: Among the Muslims of Europe and America* (1997).

Malik's work is of particular significance in that it demonstrates—in a way that echoes the pioneering work of Tariq Ramadan (Ramadan 2004)—that, for many Muslims, the emergence of British Islam is more than a historical phenomenon; it also provides the opportunity for radical redefinition:

> The enduring and often ambivalent encounter between Britain and Islam is a *fait accompli* and needs to be cherished and channelled in the wider human interest. It is not just an ideal, but an attainable objective, that Muslim intellectuals, politicians and other activists, assisted by the

more concerned and appreciative fellow citizens, should bridge the divergences so as to become the harbingers of a more vibrant form of an overdue Islamic renaissance strongly rooted in the United Kingdom. (Malik 2004, p92)

In developing his position, Malik moves beyond many other writers in considering the aesthetic and literary contributions that British Muslims are already beginning to make as part of a 'nascent intellectual tradition' (p108)—exemplified in the work of such writers as Hanif Kureishi (see 2.3), Tariq Ali, and Yasmin Alibhai-Brown. Their 'pioneering discourse', he suggests, will contribute to the 'quest for identity in the changed sociological and historical context' (Malik 2004, p119) in which Muslim communities find themselves.

A number of ethnographic studies relating to British Islam are also relevant to this study. Alison Shaw's *Kinship and Community: Pakistani Families in Britain* (Shaw 2000), focusing on the Muslim community in Oxford, is significant in providing information and detail relating to the place of the Qur'an in daily life not normally referred to in texts on Islam. A good illustration of this is Shaw's treatment of the *Khatmi-Qur'an*, a ritual in which the entire Qur'an is read, usually by a group of up to 30 individuals (often women), and which is believed to confer *sawab* (spiritual merit) on the participants:

> The recitation of the entire Qur'an is considered particularly efficacious in time of illness, risk or danger, times at which Allah's blessing, intervention and protection is most required, because the Qur'an is believed to contain an appropriate passage for every occasion. (Shaw 2000, pp249–250)[34]

Because of its part-emphasis on schooling, Ghazal Bhatti's *Asian Children at Home and at School* (1999) will be referred to in the next section.

2.6 Muslim educational life in Britain

Though standard works on British Islam make frequent reference to educational provision, and there have been attempts to survey the British Muslim educational scene in general (eg Haque 2004), the emphasis has largely been on formal schooling. There is frequently detailed analysis of the issues relating to whether Muslim schools should be granted voluntary-aided status within the public sector, itself part of the wider 'faith schools debate' (eg Cush 2005). Though Marie Parker-Jenkins has done much to raise the profile of Muslim pupils within state mainstream schools and to interpret Muslim views on education for non-Muslim educators, the emphasis again is largely on formal schooling (Parker-Jenkins 1995).

Unlike Parker-Jenkin's more general and theoretical exploration of issues, Ghazala Bhatti's *Asian Children at Home and at School: An Ethnographic Study* (1999) does provide significant ethnographic detail about Muslim family's and children's attitudes to a range of issues, including education (see also Din 2017). Even here, however, the emphasis is almost exclusively on experience within mainstream schools rather than on patterns of learning provided within the Muslim community itself.

The main focus of Greg Smith's *Children's Perspectives on Believing and Belonging* (Smith 2005) is neither on Muslim children in particular nor on their experience in supplementary schooling. Nevertheless, it does provide some valuable research data relating to the effect of attendance at supplementary schooling on Muslim children's use of out-of-school time, including time spent with others. Thus:

> [g]iven the amount of time spent in mosque it was unsurprising to find an absence of highly observant Muslim children reporting playing out, or attending secular after-school activities, or regularly viewing children's TV programmes. When they did play out it was usually with other Muslim children on the way to or on the way back from mosque. (Smith 2005, p46)

This observation, based on a range of research methods (Smith 2005, pp69), supplements the response of hifz class students in this study (6.7) to questions about how hifz studies affected the rest of their lives.

The intensity of purpose which we note during hifz class fieldwork (chapter 6: see also 7.3), was also noted by Smith amongst those children who attended mosque classes in general:

> Almost all of them accepted that this pattern of intensive and serious religious and moral instruction within a strict learning environment was a natural part of their Muslim identity, and many of them accepted and owned what they had been taught as true and worthy of obedience. (Smith 2005, p54)

Evidence suggests, however, that there is a dearth of ethnographic detail concerning Muslim children's experiences in school in general, in supplementary education in particular.[35] It is in helping to fill this gap, as well as suggesting further lines of research enquiry, that the significance of this study lies.

In the case of supplementary schooling, this paucity of material is noted in the *Final report on Complementary Schools and their Communities in Leicester*:

> [T]here is remarkably little detailed information about complementary schools and their educational agendas and, specifically, on qualitative and ethnographic aspects of these schools. (Martin et al 2004, p7)

According to Sophie Gilliat-Ray, the situation regarding Islamic colleges and dar ul-uloom is similar:

> [F]ew scholars have documented the origins, curriculum or 'culture' of dar ul'uloom and Islamic colleges, let alone begun to understand the complex social and religious processes that lead a young person to their doors. (Gilliat-Ray 2006, p3)

There are at least two key reasons to account for this paucity of detailed information.

First, there is the difficulty in identifying and quantifying its scope. For, not only might Muslim children receive their supplementary schooling in a wide variety of settings (4.2), including from tutors in their own or other's houses or in maktabs set up independently of local mosques, but also there is no system of local or national registration. As such, any attempt to estimate the number of British maktabs or pupils who attend them must, for the time being at least, be very approximate.[36] This situation might change in view of a growing lobby by some Muslim groups (eg Muslim Parliament of Great Britain 2006) for some kind of registration system in order to introduce child protection systems. Pressure might also come from those groups, such as those set up by the Home Office in 2005 (5.5, 7.5), who are interested in seeing greater cooperation and cohesion across the Muslim supplementary school sector in order to contribute towards social harmony.

Second, there is the wish of some of those who organise Muslim supplementary schooling to remain 'invisible' (Martin et al 2004, p14). The reasons for this are probably similar to those that have resulted in so little evidence being currently available about British madrasahs and dar ul-uloom. These include suspicion of the motives of researchers and a historical reluctance to become involved in wider 'political' activities, particularly amongst those groups associated with the Deobandi tradition (2.5). Though there is evidence that such groups and associated individuals are now becoming more willing to engage with the wider world (Lewis 2004), a recent research project designed to find out about religious training and formation in four British Deobandi dar ul-uloom foundered because of the inability of the researchers to gain adequate access (Gilliat-Ray 2005).[37]

2.7 A note on cyber Islam

Before the rise of information and communication technology (ICT), for academic researchers the concept of 'literature' connoted textual material, predominantly in the form of books and journals. Since the last decade of the twentieth century, however, text has been presented and distributed increasingly in electronic form. A growing amount of this 'e-literature' is located on the Internet.

This presents difficulty for the researcher in that, though textual material, as traditionally understood, might be accessed through the Internet (as in the case of electronic journals), the Internet also presents a huge and ever-shifting body of material, much of it temporary and unregulated. Nevertheless, this can sometimes provide valuable research material that cannot be accessed through traditional channels; references to the work of Madrassa Talim-ul-Islam in Manchester, for example, were accessed in this way (7.5). On the other hand, the breadth of material related to Islam and associated themes is so enormous, multi-layered and changing, that the study of 'Cyber Islamic Environments' (Bunt 2000)—including 'cyber *makatib*' (Mogra 2004, p21)—is emerging as a field of enquiry in its own right.

In the above review and analysis of the range of literature that was consulted in preparing this study, there has been a concentration on that relating to the field of Islam and Islamic education. Though the prime purpose of the next chapter is to outline and reflect on the methodology that was applied during fieldwork, there will also be further reference to literature that was consulted.

3 Methodology

3.1 Introduction

The range of research methods used in the preparation of this study will be outlined in this chapter, with discussion of some of the practical and theoretical issues that arose. There will also be reference to some of the literature that was consulted in understanding, developing and using these methods.

Following a discussion of ethnography, reflexivity and the use of the research diary (3.2), three sections describe the use of ethnographic methods in practice: in conducting life-story interviews (3.3) and during two phases of research at Balfour Road Mosque, Ilford (3.3), including fieldwork with a boys' hifz class (3.4). The chapter ends with reference to the use of photography as a research tool (3.6) and the monitoring of radio and television programmes that was carried out (3.7).

3.2 Ethnography, reflexivity and the research diary

The ethnographic research methods that underlie this thesis, and which will be described in detail in the following sections, follow in the tradition as laid down by, for example, Robert Jackson and Eleanor Nesbitt at the University of Warwick.

Ethnography, the Greek roots of which literally mean 'people writing', is a form of qualitative research that has been defined as 'The direct observation of the activity of members of a particular social group, and the description and evaluation of such activity' (Abercrombie et al 2000, p123). It has also sometimes been described as an 'interpretive' approach (Robson 1993, p18; Jackson 1997, *passim*; Nesbitt 2004, *passim*) which, at the University of Warwick, became the basis of a dynamic and multi-layered approach to the resourcing and teaching of religious education in schools (Jackson 1997, 2000).

That ethnographic forms of research have a history, with their roots in anthropology, can be seen in Clifford Geertz's foreword to Eickelman's *Knowledge and Power in Morocco* (Eickelman 1985, ppxi–xiv) (2.3). Here, Geertz traces the history of ethnographic method in terms of the relationship between the researcher and the researched. A former one-sided 'We are the knowers, you are the known' relationship had been superseded by a dialogical approach in which both researcher and researched together, in their 'anthropological conversation', make sense of the data.

The American oral historian, Donald A Ritchie, places the value of the interview situation within such a dialogical context:

> The interviewer's objective should not be to dictate interpretation through a predetermined agenda but to provide a conducive environment for a conversation that addresses relevant issues. (Ritchie 2003, p103)

In such a context, there is the potential for both fieldworker and participants 'in the field' to be enriched by ethnographic encounter; from the researcher's point of view, this was certainly the case in relation to the fieldwork underlying this study (1.2). Although, because of the context in which interviews and observation took place (3.4), it was difficult to gauge the impact of the research exercise on hifz class members, field notes indicate that life-story interviewees (chapter 4) were affected significantly by the experience. They commented, for example, on how investigation of their own life stories had prompted them to reflect on their own identity in general and the place of learning and education in their own and other's lives in particular. This confirms Nesbitt's observation that 'An ethnographic alertness helps us to see the world differently' (Nesbitt 2004, p151).

But, though potentially perception-changing, ethnography also requires both rigour and discipline, not least in addressing what is termed 'reflexivity'. Put simply, researchers are not 'neutral' but shape the research exercise in a myriad of ways: through, for example, the life-style, values, assumptions, and habitual ways of thinking that they bring to the exercise. As such, contemporary researchers recognise the need to be aware of it. Though 'reflexivity' is in itself a 'difficult and even controversial term' (Plummer 2001, p208), Nesbitt, in reflecting on her own experience of ethnographic research, expresses the core of the concept succinctly:

> Over the years I have realized more and more keenly the ways in which the researcher and the 'field' (the other) change each other. From the researcher's first steps toward formulating a research question through to the final editorial decisions on quoting interviewees and portraying their community in a report the researcher is a catalyst. (Nesbitt 2003, p47)

In short, 'ethnography requires us to be reflexive, because the ethnographer affects, and is affected by, the field' (Nesbitt 2004, p150).[38]

In order to promote reflexivity, a 'research diary'—sometimes referred to as a 'personal log'—was maintained and consulted regularly during the course of this research. This proved to be a useful tool and validated to a large extent Ken Plummer's description of the role of log books (as used in life-story research) as 'designed to convey the researcher's changing personal impressions of the interviewee, of the situation, of their own personal worries and anxieties about the research' (Plummer 2001, p152).

Following the first interview with Sam Chowdhry (4.2), for example, the diary entry was as follows, the italics indicating reflection on the (roman) text that preceded it:

> At the end of the interview, he asked me what I thought of his life-story. *A sense of needing authentication/confirmation?* (Research diary [RD] 23.8.01)

But, the research diary proved to be more than a record of impressions and concerns; it also created a space in which to record thoughts and feelings about the nature of the research being undertaken in the context of continuing reflection and background reading, as illustrated by the entry:

> It seems to me that the depth of a life-story interview enables the interviewee to begin to respond at depth, for them to begin to think through ideas during the course of the interviews, to make connections that they had not seen before or, at least, only intuited. (RD 29.5.03)

During initial fieldwork at Balfour Road Mosque (chapter 5), the following reflection was recorded:

> It is a case of creating knowledge and understanding layer by layer ie when you begin, you can only ask basic questions that evince basic answers. Having assimilated knowledge and understanding at that level, you then proceed to prod a little deeper (ie move 'down' to the next level). Doesn't Erricker [2001] make reference to a mining metaphor somewhere? (RD 24.1.04)[39]

The diary also created space in which to record and partly develop ideas and hypotheses that were beginning to emerge. Take, for example, the following two entries which demonstrate exploration of the contrast between traditional Muslim and contemporary Western models of education and how they might impinge on each other:

Re the teacher—the source of authority must be a key issue. Within traditional Islam, the teacher is valued as the custodian of that which he has had passed on to him and which he, in turn, must pass on. Can this be said of the contemporary 'Western' teacher? (RD 11.1.03)

In that the oral/aural tradition of education implies careful listening on the part of the learner/listener, is there something here for LEA schooling to reflect on (ie in the context of the frequent complaint that children's listening skills are not what they should be)? (RD 4.6.04)

Thus, the research diary proved its worth in provided a practical means of maintaining a disciplined, reflective and reflexive stance during the course of the research project.

3.3   Life-story interviews

Prior to beginning the two phases of research at Balfour Road Mosque (3.4), and running alongside the earliest work at the mosque, a series of four lifestory interviews were conducted with Muslims living in Redbridge (August 2001 to November 2003). The aim of these interviews was to ascertain the role of education and learning, particularly Qur'anic and Islamic learning during childhood, within the lives of actual British Muslims, whether or not this took place in formal supplementary classes. The formal objectives were: to familiarise the researcher with the role of education and learning within the lives of contemporary British Muslims; to learn about variety in educational practice and provision; and to involve those being interviewed in reflecting about the place of education and learning within the lives of British Muslims, including the relationship between supplementary and mainstream schooling.

There is a comprehensive literature exploring the provenance, nature, and role of researching 'life-stories', particularly in the context of oral history (eg Portelli 1997, Thompson 2000, Plummer 2001). Much of what is said is consistent with the dialogical nature of contemporary ethnographic research. Paul Thompson, for example, places the life-story interview in the context of a radical redistribution of societal power:

> [T]he nature of the interview implies a breaking of the boundary between the educational institution and the world, between the professional and the ordinary public ... For the historian comes to the interview to learn: to sit at the feet of others who, because they come from a different social class, or are less educated, or older, know more about something. (Thompson 2000, p12)

Given the wide incidence of 'Islamophobia' within Western society (1.5), in conducting the life-story interviews there was certainly a strong sense of what Plummer calls advocacy (Plummer 2001, p249: see also Russell 2006) in taking the life stories of the interviewees seriously, a sense of redressing, in some way, an historical imbalance between individuals of different cultural groups.

Given the frequently negative image of mosque classes and their methods, advocacy also expressed itself in terms of wanting to take the Islamic tradition of education seriously and to attempt to understand it on its own terms.

The four life-story interviews that took place were different from the later semi-structured interviews described in 3.5 below in three significant ways. In that they consisted of several one-to-one meetings, each of 60 to 90 minutes in duration, they had an intensity that was lacking in the more conversational and public hifz class interviews. Furthermore, in that the conditions could lead on to disclosures of a personal nature—indeed, one of the interviewees spoke about a childhood mosque incident that she had not spoken to anyone else about before (4.2, 4.6)—matters of confidentiality (including anonymity) had to be discussed as one of the range of ethical considerations that this kind of research requires. The demands on the interviewer were also of a greater intensity in that it was agreed that interviewees could review, and amend or supplement as they saw fit, the full transcripts of each interview. Plummer describes transcription as 'a hugely time-consuming—and often boring—process' which, for every hour of tape, can take up to ten hours to transcribe (Plummer 2001, pp149–150). This was borne out during the course of transcribing these interviews.

There was also the issue of what to record, including what is often called 'verbal noise': pauses, inflections, coughs and asides, and so on (see Portelli 1997, p15, pp22–23). In the case of these four life-story interviews, transcripts were edited as little as possible and thus included, for example, incomplete sentences. A note was also made of verbal noise when it was thought to be significant—'long pause' or 'chuckle', for example. Such notes helped, in part, to later recapture some of the mood of the interviewees at these points and thus allow a more nuanced reading of the transcripts.

The literature on conducting life-story interviews in general, and interviews in particular (eg Atkinson 1998), suggests a number of ploys or stratagems that can be employed. One example, suggested by Plummer (2001, p123), is to begin the first interview with a general question that could help to shape the sequence that follow. Thus, the first of the questions that each of the interviewees was asked was: 'If you could divide your life into a series of chapters, what would they be?' This gambit proved to be less successful than literature had suggested, however, in that none of the four interviewees found it easy to provide a concise list of 'chapter headings'. Nevertheless, the question—following on from a reminder of the purpose of the interview and the nature of its confidentiality, in line with ethical considerations—did serve the purpose of getting the interview process under way.

There are a number of ethical issues associated with life-story methods of research, including that of who 'owns' the material thereby produced, which Plummer describes as 'Perhaps the most crucial ethical problem in life-story research' (Plummer 2001, p222). In the case of these life-story interviews, each interviewee was given a sheet outlining the purposes of the research exercise, including a contact name and number at Warwick University in case further verification or clarification was needed, and containing a clear statement about confidentiality. With regards to the latter, discussions took place with the participants each of whom chose the pseudonym that they would like used.

Another issue concerns the reliability and validity of the data, particularly important in the context of what is known about human memory and storytelling (Plummer 2001, pp232–253). In the case of these life-story interviews, much of what was disclosed had to be taken 'on trust', though factual details were checked with interviewees (dates of family moves, or the number of siblings in a family, for instance) and attention was paid to internal consistency. In some cases, notably in the case of Sam Chowdhry's family's involvement in the social turmoil associated with the partition of India (4.2) and his later emigration to Britain, it was possible to place what was being said into a known historical framework.

Despite such issues, the life-story interview, as chapter 4 witnesses, produces material of a depth and authenticity—Colin Robson (1993, p382) refers to its 'compelling interest'—that would be difficult to obtain in other ways. Moreover, the nature of the material makes a significant contribution to the creation of what Geertz calls 'thick description', that is, information together with layers of interpretation that make its significance meaningful to the 'outsider' (Jackson 1997, p33).

The dialogical nature of the life-story interview also leads to a great sense of personal gratification intimately linked to the realisation that interviewees are sharing that which is most special: the story of their own lives. This accords with the comment of Robert Atkinson who, referring to a particular life-story that he had produced, stated that he 'felt honoured to be the recipient' of the story which the interviewee had offered him (Atkinson 1998, p79).

Ian Russell, the musical ethnographer, expresses the same kind of sentiment: 'We are privileged by being granted an insight into the life and culture of our associates—their gift to us' (Russell 2006, p27).

3.4 Two phases of research at Balfour Road Mosque

The fieldwork carried out at Balfour Road Mosque, Ilford, took place in two phases. A preliminary piece of fieldwork (September 2003–January 2004), involving a series of general visits and observations, was important in building up an understanding of the nature of the maktab as an institution: its size, constituency, educational programme, pedagogical methods, and so on. The outcomes of this piece of fieldwork are described and discussed in chapter 5.

During the first phase of fieldwork, it became apparent that certain boys undertook to learn the Qur'an by heart and that they were divided into two hifz classes. This then suggested the second phase of fieldwork, conducted between June and July 2004, which involved observation of one of the two hifz classes and interviews with many of its students. The outcomes of this piece of fieldwork are described and discussed in chapter 6.

In that gaining access to Muslim institutions such as mosque schools can be highly problematic (Gilliat-Ray 2005), both phases of fieldwork were only possible with sensitive and careful preparation. In this instance, it was through one of the mosque's imams—the same imam who had taken a lead role in the production of the *Muslim Madrassahs in Redbridge* briefing paper (1.2)—acting as 'gate-keeper' that access was possible. He liaised with the mosque committee, an influential body in any mosque, and identified which of the two hifz classes should be the focus of fieldwork. He was also allowed himself to be used as a constant reference-point during the process of research itself: to make sure that the hifz class teacher was comfortable with what was going on and that protocols were not being breached, to check on newly-encountered technical terms, and so on.

There were also ethical issues to be considered. Because willing participation in fieldwork implies an understanding of the purposes of the research exercise (BERA 1992, 7), a letter was written to the mosque committee setting out the purposes of the exercise and the researcher's credentials. Regarding the proposed interviews with the students in the hifz class, discussion took place about whether parental consent would be needed (BERA 1992, 8). It was largely in response to this issue that the imam, who had close contacts with the families from whom the students came, advised that students be interviewed within the classroom setting (see 3.5 below).

3.5 Fieldwork with a hifz class

The design proposal that was drawn up for the hifz class fieldwork worded the research question thus: what is the educational significance of the experiences in hifz class of a group of north-east London Muslim boys in mid-2004? Four methods of data-collection were proposed: general observation of the hifz class at work; semi-structured interviews with small groups of hifz class students; completion of a questionnaire by hifz class students; and, the completion of a diary by some members of the hifz class. The fact that not all of these methods were actually used demonstrates how research plans can only ever be provisional and thus can evolve during the course of their application.

General observations were conducted using a checklist so as to ensure both focus and breadth (see appendix 1). During the first observation session, a ground plan of the hifz classroom was also drawn and a record kept of movements during this and subsequent observation sessions (see appendix 2); this not only helped to decipher the different stages of activity for those students attending a session (6.4) but also provided a framework for further notes and reflections following each of the fieldwork sessions.

The title 'semi-structured', in contrast to the 'structured' interview, is used in research literature (eg Robson 1993, pp230–231) to refer to an interview that follows a sequence of prepared questions but in which the interviewer feels able to omit some or add other questions in response to the interests and concerns of the interviewees. The interview schedule that was drawn up (see appendix 3) consisted of a number of *aides memoire* arranged under three headings: 'Experience as a hifz student', 'Experiences as a hifz student in relationship to the rest of their lives and experiences' and 'General reflections'.

During the first observation session, it was suggested by the hifz class teacher that I might like to talk with individual students during the session and in the room itself. Thus, the original proposal that I meet with small groups of students away from the classroom (see above) was overtaken by events. The reality of the situation also meant that the idea of some students maintaining diaries, so that it could be seen how much time was being devoted to supplementary class-type activities, was also shelved. The proposed questionnaire metamorphosed into an information sheet (see appendix 4) that was completed with each student at the beginning of our first meeting and which included, in lieu of the diary, a question about how much time each week was devoted to mosque school-related activities. Other information included the name and age of the student, how long he had been a member of the class, and family background. Using general photographs of the hifz class at work (3.6), it was also possible digitally to insert a photograph of each student on to his information sheet, thus helping recognition during observation sessions and aiding recall during post-observation reflection and analysis.

Soon into the second phase of research, interviews with hifz class students began. In all, over the period of the observation (11 sessions, totalling 11 hours), 13 pupils were interviewed, the age range being eight to 17 (6.2). The exercise was conducted on a session-by-session basis, the teacher usually asking students, in turn, to meet with me. Thus, though the researcher's record-keeping and follow-up were precise, from the hifz class perspective there was an element of happenstance to the process. On several occasions, for example, two students were met with at the same time, simply on the basis that two came forward at the same time. From the researcher's point of view, given issues of access and the need to maintain a cooperative relationship, the hifz class teacher's suggestions were welcomed. Whenever possible, he was shown field notes that were being made, as well as photographs that had been taken (see 3.6 below), so that the research could be conducted in an open and trusting spirit (BERA 1992, 1).

Once meetings with students began, it became clear that the interview schedule was too long and, given the time available, a narrowing down of interview foci was needed. As a practical response, then, interview questions were sub-divided into three types: those that were imperative, those that were important, and those that would be useful to ask. Thus with each student, upon completion of the information sheet (see above), the questions progressed through each of these three types.

Hand-written field notes were kept during each observation session, consisting of: an annotated plan of the classroom showing timings and movements of students (see above); general observation notes based on a checklist (see above), and records of the meetings with students. As soon as possible after each observation session, field notes were word-processed. In addition, a grid was maintained showing which students had been met and which foci had been addressed. It was at this stage that the research diary (3.2) was reviewed and, if appropriate, added to, in order to maintain reflexivity and to identify and reflect on inchoate themes.

Both during the period of fieldwork, and more intensely following its completion, analysis of data took place. This included a detailed review of the notes made during interviews with students. In order to identify themes and common material, a system of colour-coding was adopted. References to 'prayer' (such as Umran's 'Praying gives you energy'), for example, were highlighted in green, students' personal reflections on the process of becoming a hafiz (such as Mukhtar's 'Sacrifices have to be made') in yellow. The collection of students' information sheets was also reviewed in order to collate material, such as family backgrounds (6.2).

3.6 *Photography as a research tool*

Literature suggests that photographs can play a meaningful and significant part in ethnographic enquiry (eg Norman 1991; Nesbitt 1993, 2001). Advances in digital technology mean that photographs can now be used in a much more versatile way. For example, photographs can be checked for quality immediately (using the digital camera viewing screen), images can be easily and speedily printed or edited using a computer, and photographs can be copied into documentary material.

As Nesbitt found (1993, pp286–287), photographs can play a varied role in ethnographic research: in supplementing field notes, for example. It was with this intention that photographs began to be taken in Balfour Road Mosque hifz class. Given the traditional Muslim predisposition against any humanly-created figurative image (including, for some Muslims, photographs), this was done only with the permission of the hifz class teacher and, even then, only infrequently and discreetly so as not to generate any sense of dis-ease.

Given the sensitivity of the situation, it was ironical that a further use of photographs soon became apparent: as a visual aid and prompt during the interviews with individual students (see photographs, appendix 6). As such, a number of photographs were taken of students sitting individually or in pairs around the circumference of the room. Others showed students sitting in front of the teacher 'reading' to him, or behind such students waiting their turn. This use of photographs as a research tool worked to a degree; they did sometimes lead to useful discussions of such matters as the significance of bodily postures and physical positioning in the room, what was taking place at different stages of a session, and the feelings of students as they engaged in different activities. On the other hand, students seemed less stimulated by them than the researcher had envisaged. This might have been a result of the stress on orality-aurality (2.4) within this setting in particular and within the Islamic tradition of learning in general.

3.7 The monitoring of radio and television programmes

In addition to review of academic texts and journals, BBC radio and television programmes concerning Islam in general and British Islam in particular were monitored between June 2004 and March 2005. As we have already noted (1.5), this was a useful way of identifying a growing interest in aspects of British Islam, such as the role of the immigrant imam, Islamic colleges, and the power of local mosque committees. It also provided a source of contemporary material, supplementing that found in academic literature and accruing from fieldwork, that might have been difficult to obtain in other ways. Material relating to issues such as the use of corporal punishment in the mosque and attitudes of Muslim youth to traditional mosque activities has already been referred to (1.6).

The progress of digital technology aided this aspect of data collection. For example, background information about BBC radio and television programmes could be accessed on the Internet and, sometimes, complete transcripts of programmes could be downloaded. Programmes could also be heard again using the BBC 'listen again' facility. This was not always the case, however. In early December 2005, for example, a programme in the BBC Radio *Air Mail* series focused on the legacy of the Deobandi movement in India and on life in Indian Deobandi madrasahs. Curiously, the BBC did not provide the usual 'listen again' facility and emails to its helpline service went unanswered.

This chapter has outlined the methodology that was used in carrying out the various types of fieldwork that are now described in the following three chapters. The first of these sets out the outcomes of life-story interviews with four contemporary British Muslims.

4 Case Study One: Life-story Images of Muslim Education[40]

4.1 Introduction

Reference has already been made (3.3) to the use of life-story methods in oral history collecting and ethnographic fieldwork. In the case of this study, life-story interviews were held with four Muslim adults living in the Ilford area of north-east London in order to learn more about the place of education and learning within the context of their total lives.

The fruits of these life-story interviews were a quantity of rich transcript material which amply achieved the objectives which have already been outlined (3.3) but which also provided a useful commentary and supplement to the historical and theoretical material that has already been reviewed and to the second phase of fieldwork to follow.

Following a brief summary of the general and education background of each person (4.2), referred to by a pseudonym of their own choosing (3.3), the rest of the chapter will draw examples from the transcript material in order to illustrate five themes: the lasting influence of a teacher (4.3); episodes on the path of Qur'anic learning (4.4); the sub-culture of mosque-based education (4.5); darker reminiscences of mosque-based education (4.6); and, finally (4.7), the contested nature of traditional methods of Muslim education.

4.2   The sample group

The four individuals—two men and two women—who agreed to be interviewed were not a precisely selected representative sample of British Muslims but, rather, were individuals who expressed a wish to be involved in the research project. One of the men (Sam Chowdhry) was not only considerably older than the others, but was also the only one to have been born in another country before moving to Britain as an adult immigrant. He was, therefore, the only one of the group not to have received an education in British schools, though his secondary schooling in Pakistan had been at an English-language missionary college. His British-born children, however, had attended English state schools and he himself had taught in a number of British schools. Each of the other three interviewees, all born between 1968 and 1972, had attended English mainstream schools.

The educational experiences of group members demonstrated amply the variety of forms that a 'Muslim education' might take, depending on factors such as family economic situation, parental preference, and reaction to particular incidents.

For example, Sam Chowdhry, who had been born in pre-Partition India and then emigrated to Britain from Pakistan in the early 1960s, had chosen to educate his own British-born children through providing them with a Muslim tutor at home. In part, this was because of his own negative experiences of maktab education as a child once his family had moved to Pakistan and could no longer afford a private tutor. But it was also because of his own critical views about methods of teaching and learning used in the classes of the mosque with which he was associated (4.7).

Case Study One: Life-story Images of Muslim Education

Gulam Ahmed, on the other hand, was born and brought up in a Muslim community in the industrial north of Britain. He went to mosque classes there, in which Gujarati was the language of everyday discourse, and, being singled out as particularly capable, joined a hifz class. He attained the status of hafiz at the age of 11. Moving to north-east London after university, he was responsible for the setting up of a small maktab in a house in Ilford though, ironically, he remained critical of the quality of maktab education in Britain (4.7).

A'isha Hussain was born in north-east London, though her parents came of northern Pakistani stock. For some years after the age of five, she was taught in Urdu at the home of an elderly female *ustaad*. Later, however, she began to attend a mosque school but her experiences in this East London mosque-based maktab so disturbed her that her father removed her. A permanent rift between the family and the mosque leaders was thereby created.

Finally, Serena Khan, with her family roots lying in pre-Partition Bombay (Mumbai) and Pakistan, was born and brought up in the outskirts of London. She had never attended a maktab but rather, together with her sisters and brothers, was taught at home by her parents:

> Everything that I learned at that stage was through them, including learning how to read the Qur'an ... and learning to read *namaz* ... fasting was always something that we grew up with and so the whys and wherefores of fasting I was, and the five pillars ... very familiar with from an early age. (Transcript of Interview [TI] 22.10.03)

4.3 The lasting influence of a teacher

All four British Muslims who were interviewed, then, had some kind of experience of Muslim supplementary education during their childhood, three of them in Britain. Though the forms that such education took were singularly different, in each case their memories of this education formed a significant part of their general memory stock. Indeed, so significant were some of the aspects or incidents associated with childhood experiences of Muslim education that their recollection, as part of this research many years later, was on occasions charged with palpable emotion. This was exemplified by A'isha's recollections of her first Muslim teacher.

As we have already noted (4.2), A'isha Hussain's first experience of Muslim supplementary education was when, between the ages of five and eight, she was taken each day to the house of an Urdu-speaking female ustaad. It was clear from her recollections that A'isha believed that this teacher had had a profound and lasting effect on her: 'there won't be one point of my life that I won't think of her'. (TI 15.5.03)

Of particular importance was what the ustaad had taught her about the significance in life of an *insaan*, the Qur'anic term for 'human being' that has played an important role in Sufi thought. It seems that the ustaad used this term to draw some kind of qualitative or even mystical distinction between ordinary people and exceptional persons:

> And she said to me … when you grow up you've got to learn to be good and you've got to learn to be an insaan. She'd always say that to me … and I always remember that, she said … when you grow up you realise that there are only a few insaans that you will meet, a few human beings … And she said when you meet people who are a real insaan, a real person, a real human being, she said you don't ever let them go. (TI 15.5.03)

So powerful was the impact on the young A'isha that, 25 years later, she could say: 'And even today, I kind of think back and I always … think, how much of an insaan am I today?' (TI 15.5.03)

Not all encounters with mosque teachers were as beneficent, however. They could be objects of fear (4.5) and encounters with particular teachers could be so disturbing that a family would decide to educate their daughter away from the mosque entirely (4.2, 4.6).

Case Study One: Life-story Images of Muslim Education

4.4 Episodes on the path of Qur'anic learning

As in many cultural embodiments of education and learning (see eg, Kane 1972, pp71–73; Eickelman 1985, pp4–5, 88–89), the different stages in learning the Qur'an can be bound up with ritual and tradition. Thus, for example, Sam Chowdhry looked back to the day when, at about the age of four or five in pre-Partition Panjab, a ceremony had been held at home to mark the beginning of his learning the Qur'an:

> The whole family was there and the imam of the mosque was there, my grandmother was there, my father was there, my grandfather was there and everyone. And there was a sweet and cooking. Like birthday party … I did feel special because I had new clothes and everything and presents from relatives … And then the *malvi*, my teacher … asked me to repeat the *kalimah*. I remembered that. Then, he had a small book, which is the Qaida, the first alphabet, and then he said, 'Okay, say *Bismillah al Rahman al Rahim*' which I did. And from there, he said he will come every day to teach me. (TI 23.8.01)

For his part, Gulam Ahmed was able to describe in great detail, and with great emotion, a significant day in his own path of becoming a hafiz. Though approximately the same age as A'isha and Serena, Gulam Ahmed's boyhood experience of Muslim education in northern England was very different. Attending a mosque school near his house, he was marked out as a gifted student at a young age and so joined the hifz class. He recalled vividly the day when, in that class, he was able to recite the final portion of the whole Qur'an that he had committed to memory:

> It's one of the most beautiful feelings that I have ever experienced in my entire life … I can picture as if it's today and it was Valentine's Day … it was a Wednesday. It's such a beautiful feeling … The whole class knows that there's something, there's a big moment here … and everyone just goes silent, as you are coming towards the end … And everyone's sat there and they know you're on the last page now. And even the teacher's

really excited ... and the teacher's sat there and he's really calm and really excited and he's got a big grin on his face ... (TI 17.7.03).

And then, once the final memorised passage had been recited, together with the opening section of the Qur'an (to show that recitation is never complete):

> Everyone congratulates you, everyone shakes hands with you, everyone pats you on the back including the teacher ... The teacher would perhaps invite other teachers within the madrasah. And everyone would come along and they'd hug you, they'd hug you with utmost reverence. (TI 17.7.03)

Throughout the Muslim world, public Qur'anic recitations are held, sometimes in the form of competitions.[41] As such, A'isha Hussain was able to recall a Sunday Qur'anic recitation competition that took place in an East London mosque in the early 1980s:

> And then, one day, we had ... on a Sunday ... we never went to mosque on a Sunday, but on Sunday we had like a competition. And our mosque used to have competitions like that where, if you learned to recite a part of the Qur'an, you'd go for this competition and ... if you read it properly, the mulvis would sit and watch you and, if you read it properly, you'd get a prize ... So ... my teacher in the mosque ... told the mulvi that ... she wanted me to go for the competition. And I remember I went and ... there were a couple of other girls ... as young as me. We went and it was really exciting and I was so excited. (TI 22.5.03)

4.5 The sub-culture of mosque-based education

Beyond these 'formal' occasions associated with Muslim supplementary education, the interviewees, through delving into their childhood memories, also revealed some fascinating details about the 'sub-culture' of mosque-based education: that is, children's experiences which ran 'beneath' or 'parallel to' the 'official' account of what was—or should have been—happening.

This was most vivid in the case of Gulam Ahmed's account of his experiences as a hifz class student. It was clear from his account that this experience was of an intensity that would probably have surprised those hifz class students who, several decades later, were observed and interviewed as part of this research (see chapter 6).

To begin with, hifz class hours were very long: including Saturday mornings and, sometimes, Sundays too: 'it was literally seven day weeks'. This had the effect, according to Gulam, of creating an exceptionally strong bond between the boys in the hifz class that sometimes led to mischievous activity in the little spare time that they could find. For example:

> I started smoking as a child when I was about nine and in those cold winter mornings a few of us would gather so I'd get a knock from one of my friends and I'd get out and, one day we're just sitting in the park, just before we're going to the madrasah and we build a little fire, just warming ourselves up and one of the boys takes out a cigarette which he'd nicked from his dad's box.

Thus:

> we were supposed to represent the pinnacle of the Islamic ideology ... So, on the surface ... when the teachers are there we are gold ... We are untainted and we are models. And yet, when we're on the out we do everything possible to try and break out of that. (TI 17.7.03)

Following this subterranean theme, Gulam also recalled what happened when new boys joined the hifz class:

> We were an exclusive club and, again, over the years ... a number of boys would drop out and a number of boys would drop in. And every time somebody comes in ... there's this little banter around 'Let's test this one. Is he up to it?' And then we have ... some of the senior ones, some of us would say 'I reckon he'll be here two weeks max. He ain't

gonna take more than two weeks'. And that was the case. I mean, so many people left within the first two or three weeks, they just couldn't take it. There was no way ... . (TI 17.7.03)

A similar glimpse into the child's-eye view of mosque education can be seen in A'isha Hussain's account of what happened when, following the death of her ustaad, she began attending girls' classes at a local East London mosque at about the age of eight or nine.

The girls' classes, it seems, were held in the lower, basement part of the mosque building. The male teachers—A'isha referred to them as mulvis—were in small rooms adjacent to where the girls and their female teachers met:

> We're sitting ... and it was a pattern, every day, we'd be talking like kids ... you'd give somebody your bubble gum ... There was a rule; everybody had to bring a sweet ... that we had to share around in our group ... we were kids—the teacher wasn't bothered with us ... We'd sit and talk. We weren't perfect saints ... When the teacher wasn't bothered, we were sitting there talking and stuff like that. (TI 22.5.03)

But, when one of the mulvis appeared, the consciousness and body language of members of the group changed radically and instantaneously:

> Then the mulvi comes and everyone is rigorously ... moving, pretending that we're reading. Suddenly all the books open ... It was a set agenda. As soon as he walks in, everyone's quiet. We're reading. (TI 22.5.03)

4.6 Darker reminiscences of mosque-based education

But such 'lighter' recollections must be balanced by reference to other 'darker' reminiscences that the life-story interviewees also chose to share.

Already, in the recollection just quoted, there is a sense of menace, power and fear in the appearance of the male authority figure. For A'isha, this was to have tragic consequences in that, following a disturbingly inappropriate encounter with one of the mulvis, her parents withdrew her from the mosque entirely in order to continue Muslim education at home.

Gulam Ahmed's own childhood experience of Muslim education also contained experience of fear. Indeed, of his own experience in hifz class, he could declare: 'I think sometimes we felt that we were in a prison'. (TI 17.7.03) Corporal punishment was, it seems, an integral part of Gulam's childhood experience of mosque-based learning:

> Most of my punishment as a child was not because of the fact that I wasn't able to learn something ... it wasn't that ... we were just naughty boys. And we used to get up to no good. And the best way to sort that out according to the teachers at the time was just to whack you one around the head or whatever ... a lot of beatings that I used to get which were with a cane, with a stick ... on my hands. (TI 17.7.05)

And parents both knew that this took place and were complicit in it: 'If I was to go home and say to my dad, "I got a real beating up today", he'd say, "Well good on you, you deserve it"' (TI 17.7.05). Indeed, so much was corporal treatment the norm that fathers would say to the mosque teacher, according to Gulam:

> Make sure that if he doesn't learn properly ... he's yours ... do whatever ... Clip him around the ear. Do whatever you need to do. Make sure that you discipline him. (TI 17.7.05)

As such, Gulam Ahmed could comment laconically: 'There was no comfort zone for any of us'.[42]

4.7 The contested nature of traditional Islamic education

In short, there was much in this series of life-story interviews—such as the place of rote learning, the power of male mosque functionaries and the frequent use of corporal punishment—to show that traditional stereotypes of mosque-based education are solidly grounded. But, at the same time, it became clear that 'traditional' methods and styles are both debated and contested from within the British Muslim community itself (1.6). Indeed, attitudes towards traditional methods of Muslim education dictated to a large extent both how and where the families from which the interviewees came chose to educate their children as Muslims.

For example, not only was Sam Chowdhry largely educated at home in India and Pakistan by a series of Muslim tutors, but this was also the method that he chose for the Muslim education of his own British-born children. To some extent this was no doubt affected by family tradition, his own childhood experiences and the financial ability to pay for tutors, but it was also informed by his extremely critical stance towards traditional mosque-based methods of teaching:

> We are actually destroying a nation ... because I have visited madrasah a few times and I don't agree what they teach, I don't agree how they teach ... To me, they are forced to sit there for two hours doing nothing and tired ... All day school and then one hour at home and then go to madrasah again and two hours there. It is too much ... Instead of teaching them Qur'an which they don't understand, my idea is that they should be taught Arabic for three hours a week, or four hours a week ... and, after five years they would be able to learn good Arabic and then they will be able to read Qur'an and understand Qur'an. (TI 6.9.01)

His own views of traditional madrasah education, then, were unambiguous: 'To me it's a punishment to the children ... it's rote learning and crude method of teaching' (TI 6.9.01).

Gulam Ahmed's childhood experiences of madrasah-style education in northern England were recollected in a stoical spirit, often infused by humour and a fondness for the past. Nevertheless, as to whether he would want his own children to experience the same: 'So if you ask me a question, would I put my son or daughter through the same—and I'd say No, I wouldn't' (TI 17.7.03).

Even though he himself sponsored a small madrasah, his views were as hard-line as those of Sam Chowdhry: 'I'm really up for reform in the

Case Study One: Life-story Images of Muslim Education

madrasahs and I think unless we reform strongly we're just gonna kill it off' (TI 17.7.03).

This response was, in part, connected with the onerous responsibility of being a hafiz within the Muslim community[43] but was also informed by Gulam's encounter in recent years with a contrasting perspective on childhood and Muslim education: that associated with Sufism. He exemplified the contrast as follows:

> [I]f I was in a madrasah and there was a gathering and a kid was playing around or something and one of the elders would jump up and clip him around the ear ... If I was in a Sufi gathering, a child would be left to do absolutely whatever he wants and for not a single person would the thought cross their mind to say "I need to discipline that kid". It's just "Let it be" ... And the child learns to discipline his or herself by watching others over time through love.

Again, in words that echo the approach adopted by A'isha Hussain's East London ustaad (4.3):

> [I]n a madrasah, the teaching ... is very mechanical, it is very much "Thou must do this, thou must do that, thou must not do this, thou must not do that" whereas the Sufi teaching is very much "God is love ... Be yourself. Don't pretend to be something you're not ... and, above all, be a human being". (TI 17.7.03)

The decision of Serena Khan's father to educate his four British-born children at home in a gentle, fairly unstructured manner was also, it seems, connected to critical views about alternative forms of Muslim education:

> [H]e'd heard about a lot of the local mosques and it seemed to be the way that most of them worked was ... if you don't do what you want them to then they will shout at you ... they may use the cane ... So it wasn't just the idea of somebody using a cane ... it was somebody other than him actually raising a finger or speaking ... in a way that was unacceptable to him. (TI 22.10.03)

Muslim Supplementary Classes

Again, as with Sam Chowdhry, there also appeared to have been concerns about the overall amount of time that young children would have to devote to education, both at mainstream school and that which followed at mosque:

> It was the fact that ... you had these small children starting off with sort-of primary and junior school that would come home from school, not even have time to rest and get themselves together and have a break and they would suddenly sort of put their get-up on as we call it and then go off on their own. (TI 22.10.03)

Serena's own views about Muslim education appear to have been affected not only by her own parents' attitudes but also by her own experience as a British state school primary teacher. As such, if she were to have children of her own:

> I would want to introduce them to Arabic at an early age ... because I'd like them to read the Qur'an. But, unlike my education, I would want them to learn to ask questions, explain the meanings of what they were reading as well and just encourage sort of general reading around Islam as well. And hopefully that would encourage them to see the benefits and to follow the faith. (TI 19.11.03)

The ways in which contemporary Muslims might have experienced education and learning, then, are many and varied. This might include attending a maktab (supplementary classes) at a mosque. In the next chapter, the structure of one such maktab is described.

5

Case Study Two: The Life and Work of Balfour Road Maktab

5.1 Introduction

So far within this study, there has been frequent use of such terms as 'Muslim supplementary education' and 'mosque schools'. This chapter will give substance to such terms through exploring the life and work of one particular example: the maktab or mosque school organised by Ilford Mosque and Islamic Society.

Because of the unregulated and variegated pattern of Muslim supplementary education (2.6), precise figures are unavailable about either how many mosque-based maktabs function within Britain or the number of pupils who attend them. Statistics such as that there are 'around 700 madrasas' (*sic*) in Britain (Muslim Parliament of Great Britain 2006, p3) or that around 400,000 Muslim children attend British mosque schools (interview with Muslim leader, Leicester, June 2005), are conjectural by nature.[44]

If statistics are hard to obtain, then there is also little if any detailed study of the life and work of actual British maktabs. As we have already noted (2.6), the same applies to institutions of higher Islamic studies in

Britain. Given this situation, though this chapter only focuses on one maktab of the many that operate in Britain today, the outline will make a contribution to the general pool of knowledge that is available currently.

Based on fieldwork carried out between September 2003 and January 2004 (3.4), an outline of the origins, nature and premises of the community (5.2) is followed by sections on maktab students and teachers (5.3), the organisation of teaching and learning (5.4) and, finally, curriculum material and approaches (5.5).

5.2 The origins, nature and premises of the community

Though general population statistics are available (1.4), no definitive study has been made of the origins, growth and composition of the Muslim community in the north-eastern London Borough of Redbridge.

From members of the current Redbridge Muslim community and a certain amount of documentary evidence, however, we do know that the community that set up 'Ilford Mosque and Islamic Society' was an offshoot of the older Ilford Islamic Centre and Mosque that continues to operate some half a mile south-east of it. Though both groups are Sunni, the latter, older community was largely Pakistani and *Barelvi* by heritage and tradition. By contrast, those members who formed the new mosque community were largely Gujarati and *Deobandi*.

In common with most other British mosques (Nielsen 1995, pp43–44), Ilford Muslim Society, the forerunner of the present Ilford Mosque and Islamic Society, sought recognition with the Charity Commission and was registered in 1985. It is significant that, in the fund-raising campaign that was held leading up to this, appeals for funds stressed community educational needs. In that the local LEA primary school hall, rented by the mosque, could only accommodate a fraction of those children who required a Muslim education, one fund-raising letter stated:

> Most of these children are without Islamic education as their parents cannot take them to other Madressahs (*sic*) almost a mile away due to

lack of transport facilities. Also, our Muslim brothers have to go for their regular prayers which at times is very inconvenient. With this need and the welfare of the Muslim children in mind our society was looking for a place where we can establish a Mosque and Madressah. (Ilford Muslim Society 1986/7)

Funds having been gathered, premises were then found—an old church hall and associated buildings in Balfour Road—and finally purchased in March 1987 (Ilford Muslim Society 1986/7). The old church hall was later demolished and replaced by a two-storey purpose-built mosque. It is this mosque, together with a converted private dwelling that it is connected to on one side and another converted house that lies a short distance away on the other (and which there are now plans to develop),[45] that the maktab uses as its premises (see photographs, appendix 5). The large room immediately above the mosque prayer hall, together with rooms in the connected building, are used for boys' classes. Girls use the rooms in the other building which, though on the mosque site, is not actually joined to the purpose-built mosque building itself.

There is versatility in how the premises are used, however. During the month of Ramadan in the year 2005, for example, the building usually used for girls' classes was used each evening by both men and boys for *tarawih* prayers.

5.3 Maktab students and teachers[46]

At the time of the fieldwork, there were approximately 300 students, between the ages of about four and 17, attending classes each weekday evening. Most attended for a two-hour session (4.45–6.45 pm), though boys in the two hifz classes had longer sessions (5.00–8.00 pm).

Students are expected to wear appropriate dress whilst attending maktab. For girls, this takes the form of a long white *jubba* (ankle-length tunic) and *hijab* (headscarf): for boys, a long white *thaub* (tunic) and white *topi* (prayer cap).

Muslim Supplementary Classes

There were some 16 or 17 maktab teachers at the beginning of 2004. All but three, both male and female, were part-time in that they taught at the mosque during each of the weekday evening sessions. The three other teachers, all male, were full-time in that teaching was only one part of their role as imams employed by the mosque management committee.

The teachers represented a variety of ages and backgrounds. Some were born in England of immigrant parents and had attended both English state schools and then, later, a Muslim college—such as the Deobandi dar al-uloom in Bury, Lancashire (Gilliat-Ray 2005, 2006). Others, however, were born elsewhere. One older male teacher, for example—the one who taught the hifz class featured in the next chapter—had been born in Gujarat, and had lived for some time in Kenya before coming to England in 1987.[47]

The different background of teachers is significant, not only for Balfour Road maktab, but also for other British mosque schools. For, as we have already noted (1.6), it is one of the key factors that affects not only the nature and the quality of education provided in general but also, because of cultural and linguistic issues, the relationship between students and teachers in particular. The management of Balfour Road maktab had taken this into account, however. For, not only was there a recognition that 'Teachers are there to give a service to the community' and that a good teacher is someone who can relate to the children (interview with two Balfour Road mosque maktab teachers, January 2004), but the deployment of teachers took notice of their background; those with less English taught the Qur'an whilst the majority who were conversant in English taught classes with the aid of English-medium text books which had replaced those Urdu books that were once used (5.5). Indeed, English has now almost totally replaced Urdu as the language of discourse.[48]

There has been a school principal at times in the history of Balfour Road maktab, as there was between 1999 and 2003. At the time of the fieldwork, however, there was no principal in post. The link between this hiatus and reported tensions within the mosque management committee was not easy to gauge for, as has been noted elsewhere (Geaves 1996, p163), it is difficult for outsiders to gain a clear understanding of the internal politics of local Muslim communities.

5.4 Organisation of teaching and learning

For a non-Muslim who has neither been schooled nor socialised within the maktab system, what takes places in the maktab appears to be, to use Østberg's phrase, a 'rather complex learning situation' (Østberg 2003, p176).

From the youngest to the oldest, pupils are divided into single-sex classes, each with its own teacher; females teach the girls and males teach the boys. As we have already seen (5.2), the separation of boys and girls is made even more obvious by the physical location of the classes. The classes are arranged according to age group, though there is some flexibility in this, particularly in the case of students who are learning either more quickly or more slowly than their peers in a particular group.

The methods of teaching and learning used in this maktab are traditional in a number of significant ways. This is most obvious in the physical arrangement of the classes. In the large room above the prayer hall, for example, four 'classes'—that is, single lines of male students arranged in semi-circles (or, more accurately, along three sides of a hollow square or rectangle), each facing a male teacher—can be seen. The traditional use of the halaqa or 'learning circle' within Islamic education, a practice said to go back to the Prophet Muhammad himself, has already been noted (2.3).

These learning circles, in which the students sit or kneel directly on the carpeted floor behind long wooden bench-like bookstands, provide the main context of learning within the maktab. At times, the teacher will address all the students in the group but, more typically, the physical layout of the halaqa enables the teacher to call students, individually or in small groups, to sit before him at the front. This one-to-one contact between student and teacher, in its classical form perceived as a teacher-to-student process of transmission (2.3), is again typical of Muslim traditions in learning and can create a strong bond between student and teacher.[49]

But if this is the most obvious *visual* context of learning in the maktab, it is the oral—or, more correctly, the oral-aural (2.4)—dimension that is more significant. For, in walking into one of the older-age maktab classes for instance, it is the *sound* of learning that is so striking.[50] Whilst one or two students might be sitting in front of their teacher at the centre front of the halaqa, the other students will be reciting out loud those Qur'anic passages that they are in the process of both committing to memory and vocalising in the proper, received manner. Many, if not most, will be doing this with their upper body moving in a bowing motion, forwards and backwards (see 6.5). Those students at the front will also be reciting Qur'anic verses out loud, in turn, the teacher listening, checking and correcting as necessary.

Within this two-fold context, of traditions relating to both space and sound, learning and teaching focuses upon four aspects of Islamic knowledge: Arabic and the Qur'an; *fiqh* (aspects of Islamic law); *sira* (accounts of the life of the Prophet Muhammad and other prophets), and aspects of Muslim practice, such as how to pray at the set time each day, and how to perform *wudhu* (ritual ablutions) before prayer.[51]

Within the younger classes, learning to read Arabic takes place in a systematic, phonetic manner. That is, the children are first taught to recognise and to write Arabic letters and then to join them together to make sounds and words. (It must be borne in mind, of course, that the children do not know what the Arabic means: only what the Arabic *sounds like* when it is read out loud.) As the older children gain mastery over reading Arabic, they begin to learn to read passages from the Qur'an and then to learn some of them by heart.

Learning to read the Arabic of the Qur'an develops along two parallel routes. First, there is the traditional task of reading through the

Case Study Two: The Life and Work of Balfour Road Maktab

whole Qur'an which might take three or four years (Redbridge SACRE 2003, p4). Second, there is the need for a Muslim to learn by heart those passages in the Qur'an that will be needed in the daily ritual life of an observant Muslim. These include those passages, such as *surat ul-Fatihah* (the opening surah of the Qur'an) and shorter surahs that come at the end of the Qur'an, that are recited (or 'read', as British Muslims often term it) daily during *namaz/salah*.[52]

The whole maktab 'year' is linked to the month of Ramadan[53] which serves as the main holiday for maktab students and teachers. In the period immediately preceding Ramadan, maktab examinations are held. The 'new' academic year then begins immediately after *Eid-ul Fitr*, the festival that marks the end of Ramadan austerities.

5.5 Curriculum material and approaches

There is at present no common curriculum used in British maktabs, a situation that some Muslim groups are wanting to change (Home Office 2005). Instead, each maktab devises or perpetuates its own. What is distinctive about Balfour Road maktab, however, is that it has chosen to follow a scheme that was developed by a South African Muslim organisation, the *Taalimi Board* (Education Board) of the *Jamiatul Ulama* (Council of Scholars/Theologians), *Transvaal* (see Mogra 2004). Balfour Road maktab has availed itself both of the textbooks produced by this organisation and of training workshops provided for teachers of affiliated establishments, of which Balfour Road maktab is one.

The textbooks produced by the Taalimi Board of the Transvaal Jamiatul Ulama (JBTJU) are English-language with the series title *Tas-heel* ('made easy'). The books are colour-coded under themes such as 'History made Easy', '*Ahadeeth* made Easy', '*Fiqh* made Easy' and '*Akhlaaq* and *Aadaab* made Easy'.

Each theme has a graded series of ten books, book 1 being the most elementary. A close examination of these books reveals a method of learning which is consistent with that linear and cumulative approach that is also a mark of Qur'anic memorisation in the hifz classes (6.4). The passages chosen to exemplify this are also a reminder of that high regard for learning and knowledge which is fundamental to the Islamic worldview (2.2).

In the 'Akhlaaq and Aadaab made Easy' series, for example, Book 1 contains a simple statement like 'Attend madrasah and please Allah' together with a story about how Shaytaan (the Evil One) loves it when his agents, the 'little shaytaan', lure children away from their madrasah studies:

> One small shaytaan says that he prevented a muslim (*sic*) child from going to madrasah. He does this by telling the child that he has to go for a haircut or go shopping etc. On this, the big shaytaan gets so happy that he embraces the small shaytaan. So one should always attend madrasah so that we please Allah Ta'ala and we do not please shaytaan. (JBTJU 1988a, p12)

By Book 7, however, statements are set within the context of a Muslim's obligation to acquire *ilm* (knowledge) and are much more developed conceptually. For example:

> Knowledge is the best of all fortune and riches and ignorance is the worst of poverty. Without ilm, a person's *Imaan* [faith] and *Yakeen* [certainty] can never be strengthened, with a result that one is deprived of action. Therefore the search for ilm is compulsory on every Muslim. Whoever has a concern for his Imaan and actions will surely make every possible effort to safeguard it no matter how much of difficulties may come his way. (JBTJU 1988b, p52)

The exercises in the books are similarly graded and, to the contemporary Western educator, would almost certainly appear limited in scope and demand on the learner:[54] from colouring in words and pictures (mosques, prayer beads and the like), through joining dots and matching sentences to completing word-searches and providing written answers to questions. Questions are almost always closed, demanding factual recall. Written answers are overwhelmingly in the form of comprehension tasks.

The earlier books in some of the themes contain 'notes to the ustaad' with advice to make things as practical as possible and to 'try to capture the interest of the children' (JBTJU 1988c, p42). In one book (JBTJU 1998d), there is even the suggestion to play games in order to make sure that children can distinguish between left and right. In that only a few of the books for the youngest children contain such explicit advice—or, indeed, any advice to the teacher at all—the implication is that serious study will concentrate increasingly on content rather than method.

This chapter has, of necessity, focused on the institutional aspects of maktab life. But what motivates children who attend classes and what do they experience? The next chapter, drawing on observations and interviews in one of the maktab's two hifz classes, will attempt to answer questions like these.

6

Case Study Three: The Experience of Hifz Students at Balfour Road Maktab[55]

6.1 Introduction

Reference has already been made both to the significance of Qur'anic memorisation in Islam and to the role and status of the hafiz in the Muslim community (2.4). It is impossible to know how many huffaz there are world-wide and the figures that are sometimes given, such as seven million (interview with two Muslim leaders, Redbridge, June 2005), are likely to be symbolic not only of the great number that there actually are but also of the vicarious pride that Muslims take in those who have followed this demanding path. Indeed, stories are told of Muslims who have achieved hafiz status in extraordinary circumstances: over a short period of time, perhaps, or at a very old or very young age, such as a South African girl who, it is said, became a *hafiza* at the age of six (interview with two Muslim leaders, Redbridge, June 2005), or the woman who memorised the Qur'an at the age of 82 (*Paigaam* 2005).

However, the status of hafiz is more than an intellectual achievement, considerable though that is; for, like Muhammad himself, through memorising its sound and text, the hafiz becomes the embodiment of the Qur'an (Gent, in publication). As such, many Muslims would not turn their back on a hafiz in that such a person has the Qur'an 'in his heart' (interview with two Muslim leaders, Redbridge, June 2005).

Across the Muslim world, there are variations in the process through which young people commit Qur'anic passages to memory. Within the hifz class described in this chapter, for instance, the students had their own copy of the Qur'an as a constant source of reference. In some other cultures such as Egypt, however, there are no extraneous aids, the student memorising the Qur'an simply through hearing the teacher recite and then repeating back until word—and sound—perfect (interview with two Redbridge Muslim leaders, June 2005).[56]

In the previous chapter, the existence of two boys' hifz classes at Balfour Road maktab was noted (5.3). In this chapter, the results of fieldwork carried out with one of the hifz classes between June and July 2004 will be set out. The nature of the fieldwork has already been outlined (3.5).

Following a description of the make-up of the target group of hifz class students (6.2), the analysis of the data gathered during semi-structured interviews and semi-participant observation will be presented and discussed so as to answer the following five key questions: how did the students come to be in the hifz class? ('Routes to the hifz class': 6.3); what pattern of operation was observable in hifz classes? ('The routines and rhythms of the hifz class': 6.4); how did the students explain the significance of what they were doing? ('The students' perceptions of what they were doing': 6.5); did striving to become a hafiz involve an element of hardship? ('The sacrifice of becoming a hafiz': 6.6); and, how did participation in the hifz class affect the rest of their lives, including school life? ('Hifz class and the rest of the students' lives': 6.7).

Case Study Three: The Experience of Hifz Students at Balfour Road Maktab

6.2 The make-up of the target group

The number of students attending the hifz class during observation sessions varied from 10 to 17. Variation in number depended on a number of factors. Two of the students who had already achieved hafiz status, for example, did not always attend.[57] Others had been excused certain sessions because of other commitments. In all, 13 students met with me during the course of the observations in order to provide background information and to respond to a series of questions, in some cases on two occasions.

The students' ages varied from eight years one month to 17 years 11 months. The average age of the group was slightly over 13½, the median age exactly 13. Three of the students were at a local authority primary school, nine were at local authority secondary schools, and one was undertaking a two-year apprenticeship.

The family backgrounds of the students not only reflected the historical development of the British Muslim community, but also the Gujarati roots of many of the families associated with Balfour Road mosque (5.2). The majority of the students' parents had roots in Gujarat, several students mentioning specific areas such as Bharuch and Mumbai thus according with known immigrant patterns (The Runnymede Trust 1977, p14). Some had been born there, families making their way to the United Kingdom via African countries such as Zambia and Zimbabwe. Two students referred to the Pakistani heritage of their parents, a third the Bangladeshi. In the case of one student, though his father had Pakistani roots, his mother was English-born and had converted (or 'reverted',[58] as some Muslims would say) to Islam.

All students were English native-speakers but family roots dictated what other language was used at home: Gujarati in most cases but also Bengali, Urdu and Panjabi. In some instances, students said that one parent was more fluent in English than the other. Some students were fluent in their heritage language, others saying that they could do no more than 'get by'. As for the students themselves, 11 had been born in or near Ilford, one had been born in Lancashire and one in the United States before moving to London six years later.

The time that students had been members of the hifz class depended entirely on individual circumstances, there being no formal age for hifz class entry. The variation was between four months and a period of well over six years.

6.3 Routes into the hifz class

In conversing with the 13 students, it became clear that there was no single route into the hifz class although there were two basic types: what might be termed 'self-selection' and 'teacher-selection'.

Typical of the former route was when a child showed interest in Qur'anic recitation at home, this was noticed by parents who encouraged him further, the parents then approaching a mosque class teacher to ask whether the child could join the hifz class. There was then an 'interview' with the hifz class teacher, during which the child recited the Qur'an. If the child's 'reading' was good enough, the child had a short trial period—often a week, but sometimes longer—before 'fully' joining the class.

There were variations on this theme, of course. Nasim (a pseudonym, like all other names used in this chapter), for example, said that he often heard tapes of Qur'anic recitation at home, particularly on a Friday when 'Mum wouldn't let you watch TV'. This stimulated his interest, as did his older brother who was already in the hifz class and 'was enjoying it'. His father noticed his interest and suggested that he learn *Surah Yasin*[59] by heart. Nasim proceeded to do this both by referring to the text and by playing the recitation on tape. His father, impressed by this, spoke to one of the imams who arranged an interview with the hifz class teacher. Subsequently, Nasim attended the evening class, first for two hours, then for two-and-a-half and, finally, for the full three hours.

Case Study Three: The Experience of Hifz Students at Balfour Road Maktab

Jamil, on the other hand, had already had his interest stimulated by family tradition: 'A lot of my cousins have been hafiz and had been sent abroad for further courses'.[60] But a turning point came for him when he went on *Hajj* (pilgrimage to Makkah) in 1997 and during which he had an auditory experience similar to that of many other Muslims[61] and others[62] down the ages (2.4). Whilst in Makkah, he heard teams of reciters in *Masjid al-Haram* (main mosque). Some of them, he said, cried as they were reciting and it 'really touched my heart'. The result was that 'I wanted to copy them'. So, he told his father that he wanted to become a hafiz, his father approached an imam at the mosque, and he joined the hifz class.

Typical of the latter route was when a child's aptitude and ability in 'reading' the Qur'an was noticed at mosque school and the teacher then suggested to the parents that the child join the hifz class which he did after an interview with the hifz class teacher and a short trial period.

Tahir, for example, said that he was approached by the headteacher—presumably one of the mosque teachers who was serving as principal at the time (5.3)—because 'he thought that my reading was good' and asked if he wanted to join the hifz class. He joined the class that same day.

In the case of Muktar, following his teacher's recommendation that he should try out the hifz class, he discussed it with his father who advised that he should. So, he had an interview with the hifz class teacher, because 'Before you start you have to be able to read it', and then joined the class.

In reality, of course, the two 'routes' into the hifz class often overlapped, as in the case of Kazim. Having read the whole Qur'an in non-hifz classes at the mosque (5.4), he had already made up his mind to memorise the Qur'an when his mosque teacher asked the students in Kazim's class who would like to 'go further into the hifz class'. Following recitation to the hifz class teacher, he then joined.

Muslim Supplementary Classes

In talking with students about how they had come to join the hifz class, the issue of whether there had been pressure on them to do so was raised; this was important in the light of a view sometimes expressed by non-Muslim local authority school teachers and Muslims themselves (4.7) that undue burdens are placed on their Muslim pupils in terms of time spent at mosque (1.6). Without exception, however, the students were emphatic that there had been no pressure placed on them to join the hifz class. Indeed, they reported that the response of family members was usually cautious in that they checked with the boy to make sure that he realised the commitment that hifz class work would involve.

Thus, Maruf denied any form of family pressure: 'With me there was no pressure'. Having himself raised the issue of becoming a hafiz, his father told him that 'there were sacrifices but that you gain rewards too'. His father was also concerned that it might interfere with Maruf's school work.

In the case of Bilal, his grandfather from India visited the family in 1995 and, hearing that his grandson had done well in the mosque examinations, 'kept saying' that he wanted Bilal to become a hafiz. But, Bilal stressed, he also said that it was Bilal's own choice.

Mukhtar's rejection of the suggestion that he might have been pressurised into joining the hifz class could not have been clearer: 'No, not at all. It was purely free will. It's not right if you are forced and not interested. You won't progress'.

This is not to say, obviously, that families and friends were not proud of boys joining the hifz class (and thereby exerting *implicit* pressure), for this is clearly a thing of great family and community pride (2.4). Abdul, for instance, said that his grandmother had wanted one of her own sons to become a hafiz but this had not happened. Consequently, she was delighted when her grandson decided on this course.

We have already recorded how Tahir joined the hifz class on the very day that he had been approached by a mosque teacher. This resulted in him being late home from mosque on that day (ordinary classes ending

Case Study Three: The Experience of Hifz Students at Balfour Road Maktab

at 6.45 pm, hifz classes at 8.00 pm) and so his mother telephoned the mosque to see what had happened. When Tahir explained the reason, 'she was happy', he said, as was his father: 'Because it's religion, most parents would be pleased for you to do it'.

6.4 The routines and rhythms of the hifz class

For much of the year, hifz class students attend the mosque class for two sessions each Monday to Friday: an early morning session of about 45 minutes (6.30–7.15 am) and an evening session of three hours (5.00–8.00 pm). During the observation period, however, the early morning class was not in session because its timing clashed with *fajr*, the first of the five set prayers of the day.

There was a measure of flexibility about which sessions particular students attended and for how long. Some did not attend the early morning session because of the distance of travel from home. As we have already seen (6.3), new students usually staggered their entry into the evening class. Some students left the evening session early because of other commitments such as school work or, in the case of Jawad, because of a mid-week football practice. The rule, in each case, was that consent had to be obtained from the hifz class teacher.

The hifz class met in an upstairs room in the converted residential building on to which the purpose-build mosque prayer hall had been built some fifteen years previously (5.2: see appendix 5, photograph 2). The small room was rectangular in shape with two windows, overlooking a residential street, on one side. Furnishings were, from a non-Muslim Western perspective, sparse; there was wall-to-wall carpeting with a smaller rug laid on top, touching the wall at the end that the teacher sat, but leaving a border on the other three sides. Of the three types of furniture in the room, one type was more significant than the others: the six wooden 'benches' used by both students and teacher, sitting alongside them on the carpet, on which to rest their copies of the Qur'an (see diagram, appendix 2). The other two pieces of furniture, a small filing cabinet and a fan, were purely functional. Except for a blackboard on the wall against which the teacher sat (and which was not used during the period of observation),[63] the walls of the room were bare.

The physical positioning of the teacher and students was both significant and functional (see appendix 7, photograph 1). The significance lay in the positioning of the teacher in relation to the students. Only the teacher, who was addressed and referred to as *Malvi Sahib* by the students (but sounding, to the untutored ear, more like *Mow Saab*), remained in the one place during classes, sitting on the rug with his back against one of the walls, with a single wooden bench in front of him, so that he could easily see all students in the room. This both established his position of authority within the group but also meant that he could keep a watchful eye on students, intervening, coaxing or chiding when he thought it necessary.

To understand the functional aspect of the positioning of students, it is necessary to understand something of the 'rhythm' of learning that shaped the life of the hifz class student.

Each student, at his own pace,[64] was working through the 30 *juz* into which the Qur'an is divided. The ideal is both sequential and cumulative. So, for example, a student might memorise a sequence of verses in the juz he had 'reached' during the early morning session: 'It's easier to learn in the morning', Umran said, expressing a traditional view.[65] Then, arriving at the evening session, he would spend the first part of class going over those 'new' verses, reciting them out loud to himself to make sure that they had been remembered. At this point, he would be sitting 'off' the rug, facing one of the side walls with a bench in front of him (see appendix 2; appendix 7, photograph 2). When he felt he was ready, he would then go to the teacher,[66] handing him his copy of the Qur'an open at the section he had learned, and recite the verses. In that there were other students also waiting to recite to the teacher, a 'queue' formed on the mat in front of the teacher's bench. Whilst they were waiting to be heard, students would continue reciting their memorised verses, using the Qur'an as a check and a guide (see appendix 7, photograph 3).

Once a student had been heard for the first time, with or without verbal corrections by the teacher, he would then return to sit in front of one of the side benches in order to 'revise' the section of the sipara immediately preceding the new verses that he had just recited. When he was once again confident that he had remembered these, he would then either go directly to recite to the teacher or form part of the queue of students waiting to be heard.

Once the second visit was complete, the student would then revise a part of the Qur'an that had been memorised at an earlier date, the 'completed' (that is, already memorised) sections of the Qur'an being worked through section by section. Again, he would recite these verses to the teacher.

Thus, in terms of the student's experience, each evening session was divided into three parts,[67] each part consisting of oral revision followed by recitation to the teacher. The system, as Boyle points out (2004, p26 & *passim*), is much more akin to a traditional apprenticeship model of learning, in which mastery is emphasised, than to current styles of Western non-Muslim schooling.

That this is an ideal can be shown in the case of Nasim, however. Like many of the students, Nasim maintained a written record of his progress on specially provided 'Notes' pages in his copy of the Qur'an. A review of these notes showed that he had started in the hifz class on 9 December 2002. He had completed the first juz by 24 February 2003, had completed the first half of second juz by 4 April, and the whole of the second juz by 19 May. But then the list showed that on 30 September, by which time Nasim had completed three and a half juz, he had 'stopped for *dhur*[68] for two months'. One of the imams explained that, if a student was beginning to forget sections of the Qur'an learned at an earlier stage, the teacher would halt his progress for a period in order for him to go back through those earlier sections so as to consolidate his memory.

6.5 The students' perceptions of what they were doing

As can be inferred from the above, membership of the hifz class involves an extraordinary degree of commitment from students (6.6). But why did the students want to become a hafiz in the first place? This central question occupied a major part of discussion with the students.

Considering the age range in the class and the subtlety of the question, it is not surprising that student responses varied in terms of depth, breadth and detail. It is useful, none-the-less, to categorise their responses in terms of 'religious', 'social', 'educational' and 'personal' reasons. In using these categories, however, two caveats are needed. First, whereas to the Western, secularised non-Muslim, the category of 'personal' might appear as logically prior to the others, the order used has been chosen so as to be more faithful to the Islamic tradition and world-view. Second, it is important to remember that all such distinctions are artificial and that, in substance, all responses related to key Islamic beliefs and values.[69]

'Religious' reasons, those in which explicit reference was made to Islamic doctrine or beliefs, predominated and were usually the most substantial. At its most general, there was reference to the 'blessings' that accrued to both self and others from learning the Qur'an by heart. There were, however, a number of specific references to the Hereafter. Kazim, for example, stated that 'We believe that if you become a hafiz, you go to Paradise'.

Some other students developed this further by stating that entry to Paradise was not only assured for oneself but also for others: 'When you pass away, you can take seven generations with you to heaven' said Hassan. But there was strong evidence that this was not understood in purely instrumental terms: that hafiz status *guaranteed* entry to Paradise. Both Maruf and Jamil expressed this in their own ways: 'If you have

Case Study Three: The Experience of Hifz Students at Balfour Road Maktab

become a hafiz *and have been good*, it's good for you on the Day of Judgement' (Maruf: stress added) and 'When you get old and go to heaven, you are allowed to take a certain amount of people to heaven—*but only if you have been a real hafiz*' (Jamil: stress added).

Another particular reference made by several students was to preserving the Qur'an, interesting in that the Arabic verbal root of 'hafiz' means, amongst other things, to 'preserve' (2.4).[70] Rafiq, for instance, made a reference (in a way that invited comparison with Ray Bradbury's novel *Fahrenheit 451*) to a story about an attempt to destroy all copies of the Qur'an but this had been impossible because, in the case of those who had memorised it, it was 'in people's hearts'. A variation on this theme was the focus on preserving the text/sound of the Qur'an as in, for example, Jamil's assertion that 'There will always be at least one person who can read the Qur'an. This will prevent those people who want to change it'. Other more personal religious reasons included Tahir's 'It is better for you as a person because you know the whole religion. When you become a hafiz you remember God more' and Mukhtar's 'it brings me more closely to my religion'.

Social reasons for becoming a hafiz were all related to the esteem in which the hafiz is traditionally held within Muslim communities (2.4, 6.1). Thus, the 'respect' and 'status' that would come with achieving the position of hafiz were referred to as were the pride that parents and family would take, even more so in the case of Hassan, because 'There is no-one in my family who is a hafiz'.

Several students offered reasons relating to education and learning. At its most general, Umran expressed his response as a truism: 'It's better to push your education further, isn't it?' But other responses were cast within an Islamic mind-set. Jamil, for example, said that 'You don't just do it for yourself ... someone who doesn't know how to read, you can help them to do this stage'. The reference to 'stage' here is explicable in terms of the immediately preceding focus of our conversation in which Jamil had explained that becoming a hafiz was a kind of 'bridge' between learning how to read the Qur'an and going on to higher Islamic studies. This simile had apparently been introduced to him by his cousin, himself a hafiz.

Finally, several students responded in terms of personal factors. Abdul, for instance, said that becoming a hafiz affected him as a person through making him feel 'clean inside', giving him 'a sense of peace' and by making him 'stronger inside'. Mukhtar, by contrast, said that it 'feels like you're achieving something'.

But, if these were the kinds of reason that students themselves gave in trying to explain what they were doing, both their language and their physical appearance were indicative too.

That memorising and reciting the Qur'an is seen as a devotional activity, that reciting the Qur'an is in fact a form of worship, was indicated by the use of the concept of 'prayer' by a number of students. In talking about what happens at both morning and evening sessions, for example, Rafiq said that he would 'pray a new page' in the former and 'pray one quarter of a *juz*, including the passage learned in the morning, in the latter. On being shown a photograph (3.6) of a student reciting to the teacher and asked to explain what was happening, Maruf said he 'was praying to him and had to think quite a lot—to pray what [he had] learned before'. On being asked directly about the use of the word 'praying' in this context, Abdul's explanation could not have been clearer: 'When we're reading the Qur'an we're praying—it's worship'.[71]

The devotional dimension of what was taking place in the hifz class was also shown by the dress worn by students: the topi and the thaub (5.3). But, at a slightly more subtle level, it was also shown by the physical position that students adopted whilst reciting the Qur'an: the kneeling position that is also one of the three basic positions of salah. The extent to which the rocking motion that both teacher and students adopted, so reminiscent of *dovening* within the Jewish tradition, was a devotional as well as a mnemonic device is a tantalising one. Kristina Nelson, who

Case Study Three: The Experience of Hifz Students at Balfour Road Maktab

herself learned to recite the Qur'an as part of her fieldwork in Egypt (2.4), suggests that it is a generic aid to memorisation:

> Rocking is especially characteristic of anyone reciting a memorised text. From my personal experience, it seems to be related to the memorising process. (Nelson 2001, p112)[72]

6.6 The 'sacrifice' of becoming a hafiz

For a young Muslim to aim at becoming a hafiz is no mean decision; not only will this involve years of attendance at classes and practice outside class hours, but also the continuous intensity of the work is highly demanding and requires extraordinary personal discipline.[73] Like other human endeavours which require intense and extended personal commitment, not all people who set out on the path to become a hafiz arrive there.

The students in the target group, however, were fully aware of the demands of the path that they had chosen. When asked which kind of work was hardest—school or hifz class—Mukhtar had no doubt: 'Hifz, but sacrifices have to be made'. Kazim also used the language of 'sacrifice' in saying that, even when you were tired after school, 'you have to sacrifice in coming to the mosque'.

Several students said, however, that once a person got used to the routine, it became easier. But that there were still difficulties to be encountered was illustrated by each of the two students who had recently become huffaz. Bilal said that he had sometimes felt very low—'I never thought that I would finish'—but that he had been 'encouraged to stick at it'. Abdul, on the other hand, stated that 'It's easy to learn it but it's hard to remember it'.[74]

That there was also a different kind of demand placed on people aiming to become huffaz, the demand of becoming a *certain sort of person*, was also referred to by a number of students in response to the question, 'What are the qualities of a good hifz student?' Though there were references to such things as having a good memory and 'reading' regularly, by far the greatest number of references was to spiritual qualities such as commitment and dedication (a group of students saying that, of the two qualities *will* and *memory*, the *will* was the most important), intention (a rich concept in terms of the key importance for Islamic devotion of *niyyah*) and respect for Islam. There were also references to moral and social qualities related to the Muslim concept of adab (5.5), such as: acting as a role model for others, including younger children; acting in a respectable manner; showing respect for elders; avoiding bad influences; and using no bad language. Regarding the latter, Maruf said of the person who is learning the Qur'an but also swearing: 'If he is swearing outside, he is using the same mouth to pray the Qur'an'.

The notion of both self-discipline and sacrifice assume even higher relief with the realisation that, in both a profound and a practical sense, becoming hafiz is not only an end, but also a beginning. Both Bilal and Abdul had recently finished memorising the Qur'an and, in mid-May 2004, had both recited the final verses in front of the male congregation after Friday *jumma* (congregational) prayers. (Their recitation had also been broadcast over the mosque-home receiver system so that those at home could hear it too.) Following their recitation, there had been hugs, hand-shakes and the giving of money followed by a meal at the mosque. In the evening, there was a meal at Abdul's house for family and friends as well as mosque teachers. Later still, the boys were presented with framed certificates. But, in the midst of all this celebration and sense of achievement (described by Bilal as an 'amazing feeling'), Abdul recalled, 'Then I realised what I had taken on and what I have to do now'. For, he now saw clearly that he was faced with the responsibility, not only of *being* a hafiz, but also of *behaving* like a hafiz. And more than this; the Qur'an had been memorised but, unless it was repeated ('read' or 'prayed') regularly, the memory would fade. As Bilal eloquently put it: 'The easiest thing is to finish but the hardest thing is to remember', a comment reminiscent of the Muslim poet who declared: 'I memo-

Case Study Three: The Experience of Hifz Students at Balfour Road Maktab

rised the Qur'an. Then I forgot the verses and remembered the words' (Geertz 1976, p1492).

For the non-Muslim, the commitment, effort and single-mindedness required of those setting out to memorise the Qur'an by heart might be difficult to comprehend. In the non-Muslim world, a helpful analogy might be that of the marathon runner. Most hifz class students found it a helpful image although one student quickly identified its limits. Maruf said that the image was indeed helpful but reflected that the marathon runner is training for the 'big day' whereas, for the hifz student, 'in the mosque every day is a big day'. And then, he added sagely, 'You can't retire as a hafiz'.[75]

6.7 Hifz class and the rest of the students' lives

We have already noted (2.6) the results of recent ethnographic research which suggested that, for some Muslim children, the time spent at the mosque had marked effects on their capacity to make relationships with others during out of school hours (Smith 2005). However, none of the hifz students expressed overt concerns about the impact on the rest of their lives.

This might have been due to interview conditions (3.5) but also, perhaps, because of the firm yet flexible stance that the hifz class teacher appeared to take, particularly with older students as secondary school coursework requirements began to impact on their time. With the latter, the rule seemed to be that, as long as they showed commitment and carried on with their 'reading', they could miss certain classes or leave early on occasions.

It must be said, of course, that in view of the close relationships between teachers, students and family networks, the opportunity for students to take advantage of the flexibility that there was would be somewhat limited. Rafiq said that the relationship between student and teacher was usually good because 'all three parties [that is, student, teacher and parents] are involved', Bilal saying that the teacher became like a 'third parent'.

But what, in the perception of the students, was the effect of this 'sacrifice' on the rest of their lives? Were they conscious of 'losing out', particularly in relation to non-Muslim school friends? There was ambivalence on the part of one or two students, but the overwhelming response to this latter question was that they were not. When asked if there was ever a conflict between hifz class and school work, for example, Iqbal's response was, 'No, there's time to do things for school too'. Umran made an interesting differentiation, saying that hifz class was different to school and that 'Praying gives you energy'.

Indeed, a number of students said that they had found that they could apply memorisation methods and recitation techniques developed at mosque to their school work. Maruf, for example, referred to school GCSE English speaking and listening exercises and said that these were 'certainly easier than if I hadn't been in hifz class'. Several others spoke about how, in memorising things at school, they used the same kinds of repetition and visualisation techniques that they had learned at mosque. For example, Kazim said of a science test that he had taken at school, 'I thought of the image of my notes'.[76]

Chapters 4 to 6 have outlined and analysed the fieldwork that is at the heart of this thesis. Chapter 7 will build on and develop this through placing the fieldwork in a larger frame of reference: that of the wider social and educational community.

Muslim Supplementary Classes Within the Wider Social and Educational Community

7.1 Introduction

Following the detailed presentation of the outcomes of three types of fieldwork (chapters 4–6), this chapter will address and develop some of the larger issues already touched on at the beginning of this study, particularly in 1.8. The aim is to explore what it would mean for Muslim supplementary classes to be seen not just as a part, but a valuable and important part, of the larger social and educational community.

Articulating the value of maktab education for the students themselves and to the wider community is problematic in that creating a list of propositional statements, for example, does not do justice to the multi-faceted nature of the situation. The metaphor of 'capital', in various combinations, is therefore used in section 7.2 as a vehicle for presenting a more holistic approach.

Section 7.3 then draws on a small-scale experiment that took place in Redbridge in 2004 to test the hypothesis that there would be value in mainstream local authority teachers and those involved in maktab teaching in observing each other in order to encourage reflection on the nature and effectiveness of teaching and learning. Following the suggestion that such an exercise could give rise to the challenging of some time-honoured practices, 7.4 exemplifies this through a brief exploration of the history and significance of memorisation in learning. The chapter ends (7.5) with a brief survey of some of the factors that might promote or inhibit maktab education from being seen as an important part of the larger social and educational community.

7.2   The value of Muslim supplementary classes as 'capital'

Laying aside issues concerning current imperfections in the system (1.6, 4.6, 4.7), what might attendance at a maktab, like that illustrated in chapters 5 and 6, offer students? Or, in current educational parlance, what 'value' might be 'added' to the life of such students?

Drawing from the fieldwork findings outlined in chapter 6, such value can be expressed in various ways. For example, it is clear that students in the hifz class were encouraged to develop an extraordinary level of personal commitment, industry and tenacity: so much so that an analogy with marathon runners became helpful (6.6). The extent to which this benefited students in their non-Muslim school studies is an issue that calls for further research (8.3).[77] Again, from the hifz students' responses to the question of why they had chosen to take the arduous journey to hafizhood, it was clear that they had developed impressive levels of personal piety. This was at least the case as articulated to the researcher, in their 'dominant' as opposed to their 'demotic' discourse, to reapply Baumann's terms (Baumann 1996); devoid, that is—as it necessarily was, given the conditions under which the interviews took place—of any exploration of the 'sub-culture' of mosque-based education (4.5).

But, in order to develop a fuller, more rounded and less atomistic understanding of the value of Muslim supplementary education for both individuals and the communities to which they belong, it will be useful to draw on the concept of 'capital', albeit in an exploratory way in the context of this thesis.

Though there was resistance initially to the use of the concept of 'human capital' outside the sphere of economics (Becker 1992) and some have noted obfuscation through over-use of the capital metaphor (eg Portes 1998, p2), the use of various kinds of capital—human, social, cultural, intellectual, spiritual, political, and so on—has become widespread over the last half-century. Not only, for example, has the concept of 'social capital' become a familiar term in social science (Iannaccone & Klick 2003), but it has also been widely used in popular writings (Portes 1998), such as in the work of the American social commentator, Robert Putnam (eg 2001). Within the educational field, the concept of social capital has been used to investigate such issues as US high school dropout rates (Coleman 1988) and the educational attainment of Canadian immigrants (Hébert, Sun & Kowch 2004). Bourdieu (eg 1986) famously used the concept of 'cultural capital' in his trenchant criticism of received patterns of educational provision. In recent years, there has been a particularly interesting debate about the use of the concept of 'spiritual capital' to highlight the impact of beliefs, values and a sense of purpose not only on individual well-being (eg Zohar & Marshall 2004) but also on the economic dynamism and prosperity of particular societies and cultures (eg Berger & Hefner 2003).

In terms of the current study, 'capital'—defined here as assets and resources which are acquired and that can be drawn on for potential benefit or advantage—is a useful metaphor in at least three ways. First, it is a reminder that there are many forms of 'asset' beyond the physical, perishable, and financial. Second, it encourages the application of material and insights from across a range of traditional disciplines, such as economics, religious studies and social science. Third, it is a means of identifying ways in which participation in a social network acts as a resource for individuals and has an effect on their activities, relationships, expectations and goals. As such, different forms of capital might be utilised to identify some of the value for students of participation in Muslim supplementary education.

'Social capital', for example—a term already used by both Eickelman (1985, pp64–65) and Boyle (2004, p36) to express the value of Qur'anic learning within traditional Moroccan society—captures the sense that Muslim students are fulfilling a community expectation, and thus creating what Coleman (1988, S107) terms 'intergenerational closure'. Those in hifz class are striving to achieve the honoured status of hafiz (2.4, 6.1), a signal of mastery of socially valued attainment and knowledge, with all its attendant ceremony and tradition (4.4, 6.6). But they are also, at one and the same time, taking on a commitment in terms of both their participation in the ongoing life of the community and their personal appearance, behaviour and character (6.6). It means that they will be able to play a key role in community religious practice, such as that connected with daily salah and the round of intensive activities associated with Ramadan (2.4), thereby increasing their sense of solidarity and trust with other members of the *umma*, local, national and world-wide.[78] But, beyond strictly 'religious' practice, the trust that is inherent in the relationship with both the extended family and the wider Muslim community means that they, particularly those who have become huffaz or serve as imams, will be in a position to both contribute and gain in other ways, too. These might include, for example, officiating at the opening of new businesses or enterprises or, on a more personal level, advising families concerned about the behaviour of their children. In terms of 'gain', an imam might be offered money towards a house purchase, office accommodation to support non-mosque activities, or be given gifts. Further research is needed in order to identify the extent to which the hafiz within contemporary Britain, or indeed Europe (1.5), is combining traditional roles with newer ones which answer the evolving needs of British and European Islam (8.3).

The extent to which there is also social and cultural capital to be 'drawn on' by the wider, non-Muslim community is a key issue. That there are some students who attend Muslim educational institutions who see their role as extending beyond the Muslim community has already been noted (1.5). Within Redbridge, one of the imams of Balfour Road mosque has taken a lead role in setting up a secondary school 'community forum' that provides and trains mentors to coach older students across a wide range of ethnic groups.[79] He also hosts groups of mainstream school pupils at the mosque and involves older maktab students in, for instance, demonstrating Qur'anic recitation and the physical positions adopted during salah. In such ways, the wider community as well as the Muslim gains from the 'investment' that has been placed in this individual.

The elasticity of a term like 'spiritual capital' means that its use as a metaphor in exploring the role of mosque education can be developed in a number of ways. Following Zohar & Marshall (2004), for example, it can be used to focus in on that sense of purpose and meaning in life that was so evident in the response of hifz students in the field study (6.5). It is significant that Boyle (2004, p83) sets the outcomes of the process of memorisation in such a spiritual, life-directing context:

> Qur'anic memorization ... is an educational process whereby the Qur'an becomes embodied within the person of the memorizer, usually a child. Memorization, in this case, is a process that seamlessly unites the physical and the mental in the formation and enactment of religious and cultural practice. Seen in this light, memorization is more than the following of tradition, more than sustained discipline or indoctrination, and even more than the passing on of religious rituals. The embodied[80] Qur'an serves as a source of ongoing knowledge and protection to the child as he/she journeys through life. (Boyle, 2004)

Elsewhere, Boyle uses the metaphor of the 'moral compass' (Boyle 2004, p131: see 7.4 below) to articulate the sense of direction that Qur'anic school education can develop in a child.

Ideally, then, participants in mosque classes will develop a purpose, meaning and direction to their lives; they will be provided with a framework (based on shariah in general, and on a particular Muslim tradition, such as Deobandi, in particular) with which to interpret their own lives and those of others; they will be given a way of life (including appearance, manners and customs) that will shape their daily living; and they will develop an emotional attachment to the teaching and practices of their community. Following Berger and Hefner (2003), however, the scope of spiritual capital becomes global in that, taking the lead adopted by classic social theorists like Max Weber, they raise the issue of the extent to which this form of capital effects the economic prosperity and democratic leanings of whole societies. Thus, they suggest, the 'most urgent question at the heart of the concept of spiritual capital' is 'the varieties of spiritual capital, and their implications for market dynamism and democratic freedom' (Berger and Hefner 2003, p6). From the basis of this study alone, it is impossible to proffer a response to this question.

Finally, the inherent flexibility of the metaphor of 'capital' can be seen when used to explore the thesis that mosque school, at best, can equip students with 'educational' or 'intellectual' capital. As we have already seen in the review of the Islamic approach to knowledge, education and learning (2.2) and in hifz class fieldwork (6.5), a range of attitudes towards learning is fostered. These include the belief that the quest for knowledge is a religious duty (2.2), that learning requires certain habits or dispositions (adab) (5.5), and that the purveyor and transmitter of knowledge, the teacher *qua* alim, is to be honoured (2.2). But, in addition to such attitudes, there is a range of skills, such as the ability to speak or recite in a public setting, that is acquired within the mosque setting and which might well be transferable to other settings. The most obvious of these, and perhaps the most surprising in view of prevailing Western attitudes, is the capacity to memorise. This is of such significance that it will be treated in some depth below (7.4). Though the outcomes of ethnographic research particularly that carried out under the auspices of the Leicester Complementary Schools Trust (1.8), already suggest that

Muslim supplementary education does accrue intellectual or education capital, this is an area which requires further research (8.3).

7.3 Muslim supplementary classes within the wider educational community

The preceding section suggests that, at best, young Muslims participating in mosque-based supplementary education are provided with a range of capital 'assets' that have 'currency' both within and outside the confines of the mosque classroom. In this section, the notion that the institution of Muslim supplementary classes could develop a symbiotic relationship with the wider educational community will be developed.

At its broadest, the hypothesis is that if—rather than being considered an aberrant, outmoded or wayward species of educational activity—Muslim supplementary education were considered a significant component of the larger educational community, then this would bring benefits for both Muslim supplementary education and the other participants within that community, particularly mainstream schools.

This might be best illustrated through a small experimental exercise that took place in the London Borough of Redbridge in 2004.

Given the trust and relationship that had been built up during the two phases of fieldwork (3.4), it was possible to explore with several Muslim leaders the notion that there might be benefit in Muslim mainstream school teachers and Muslim supplementary class teachers meeting and/or observing each other at work. The underlying principle was that both forms of education belonged to a particular tradition, each with strengths and weaknesses: as such, each tradition could 'learn' from the other.

In order to test the hypothesis, two Muslim women, each with qualified teacher status and working in the mainstream primary school sector, were invited to visit and observe girls' classes at Balfour Road mosque for an hour one evening. A preparatory meeting was held so that the shape and purpose of the experiment could be discussed and an observation schedule—covering physical environment, ethos/atmosphere, relationships, teaching methods—agreed.

Following the observations, both teachers declared that they had found the exercise useful and rewarding: not only as educators, but also as British Muslims continually reflecting on their personal identity. Some of the notes made by one of the observers—Serena Khan (see chapter 4) who, because her parents had taught her at home (4.2), had never been to a maktab before—are worth quoting from in order to give the sense of the tenor and outcomes of this exploratory exercise.

Regarding the ways in which the ethos/atmosphere was like that in her own mainstream school classroom, she noted:

> Children focus on main task/activity. Good rapport between teacher and children—in that children are clear about why they are there and what they must do.

And, ways in which it was unlike her own classroom:

> Children appear to be 100% clear about why they are there and what is to be gained—they see their learning as having a direct effect on the way they will live their life and in the Hereafter.

Regarding the ways in which teaching methods were similar to the ones that she used in her own school:

> Difficult to comment on, all sessions involved children engaged in independent work, although in early years group reciting/repeating teacher. More one to one with the teacher who informed us she tried to spend at least 10–15 [minutes] with each child.

These methods were different to those used by herself at school in that 'I tend to use more group work participation to support learning'.

The observation schedule also encouraged reflection following the observation. When asked whether there was anything that she had observed that might be applied to her own classroom setting, Serena stated,

Muslim Supplementary Classes Within the Wider Social and Educational Community

'More time to carry out one to one teaching/assessment ... maybe more hours in the day!' Her next reflection drew from the sense of meaning and purpose that she had detected in the girls' mosque classes: 'There was no feeling of oppression' she had commented verbally. Thinking of her own mainstream school setting, then, she said that there was a 'Need to find a way to give children a clearer/real purpose for why they are in school and the benefits of this'.

Her final thoughts and reflections showed that Serena was already thinking through how such an exercise might be developed further: 'I feel it would be beneficial to observe boys' experience in this setting to see how similar/different their feelings are'. Furthermore: 'The above is based on an hour's observation—would findings change after several further observations?'

On a very limited scale, then, this exercise provided intimations of what might be forthcoming from a larger-scale and more thorough-going exercise in which teachers from different educational settings observed each other and, through so doing, were provided with fresh, perhaps even novel, perspectives on education in general and on pedagogy in particular.

This exercise, of course, was very small-scale and many other types of activity could be designed with more participants, planning and time: observations involving both Muslim and non-Muslim teachers, seminars bringing together Muslim teachers from mainstream and supplementary settings, meetings involving Muslim teachers from a range of maktabs, and so on. In each case, though, the underlying principle would be the same: that bringing together educators from different settings in order to share educational traditions and practices could lead to better understanding and, ultimately, better pedagogy. Within the larger educational community, such a practice would not appear unusual in that this kind of activity is a central feature of 'networking' which is seen increasingly as a spur to professional development and increased competence (1.7).

It remains to be seen what the outcomes of such encounter and dialogue would be. It could include, for example, fresh insights into: the role and status of the teacher, the determinants of pupil behaviour and attitudes towards learning, the merits of independent learning and individual coaching as against group activity, and the effects of culture and tradition on learning and teaching (including single-sex as opposed to mixed gender settings).

But, in order to develop this hypothesis further, let us examine further a pedagogic method that has remained dominant within the Islamic educational tradition though currently out of favour in English educational practice: memorisation (and its twin activity, recitation).[81]

7.4   The place of memorisation in learning

In a seminal piece on *Memory, Imagination and Learning*, Keiran Egan notes the current:

> ambivalence[82] about the place of memorisation in education. A prominent theme of the progressive movement—one that has become a commonplace of modern educational discourse—is that simply insuring memorisation of knowledge is likely to be educationally useless. (Egan, undated)

And yet, as Frances Yates (1966) has demonstrated, memorisation has had a distinguished place within Western philosophical and theological traditions. Because of the 'respect accorded in antiquity to the man (*sic*) with the trained memory' (Yates 1966, p16), tales were told of those who had shown remarkable feats of memory. From early medieval times onwards, scholars and mystics such as Augustine, Aquinas, Petrarch, Lull, Camillo, Bruno,[83] Ramus, Fludd and Leibniz spent considerable energy in exploring the role of memory in enabling people to better comprehend the nature of the world (Yates 1966, *passim*; Manguel 1997, pp55–65).[84]

Within Western educational systems, too, memorisation has also occupied a key place:

> Until the past few generations in the west, and still in perhaps most of the world today, academic practice has demanded that students in class 'recite', that is, feed back orally to the teachers statements ... that they had memorised from classroom instruction or from textbooks. (Ong 1982, p56)

Why, then, does memorisation seem to occupy such a minor place in the educational tradition represented in the contemporary British mainstream school? Though pupils might still be required to learn numerical tables and commit the words of songs or play scripts to memory, particularly when preparing for tests or public performance, learning 'by heart' occupies a very minor role in literacy and other parts of the curriculum.

A number of reasons can be conjectured to explain this departure from historical precedent. The range of textual and other resources available, for example, means that there are ample ways in which information can be 'looked up'. Again, memorisation and recitation might simply be considered 'unfashionable', redolent, as they are, of earlier, less sophisticated social conditions and needs. Egan (*op cit*) also suggests that the information explosion has fostered a process view of education: the view that education should concentrate on developing skills of access rather than knowledge itself.[85]

But there might well be a further deeper and more substantial epistemological reason, one that is highlighted through comparison with the learning tradition represented in the mosque school hifz class (chapter 6). The conjecture is that, within the context of Western secularism and modernism, there has been a profound loss of confidence in identifying key words or texts as sources of 'truth'. For, to commit something to memory, particularly a passage of text, suggests that it is of more than passing significance: that it is of such lasting significance that it is worth committing to memory so as to be available to the learner upon recall thereafter.

Given the significance of the Qur'an, sound and word, within the Islamic tradition, it is easy to understand why there are no such scruples over memorisation as a process. For, the Qur'an, as the final and complete revelation, is *de facto* worthy of being committed to memory; indeed, its accurate transmission from the time of Muhammad onwards *required* that such a process took place (2.4). As such, as we have already stated (2.4), it would be both misguided and reductionist to suggest that Qur'anic memorisation is 'merely' a relic of the need in pre-literate and proto-literate societies to remember words in the absence or scarcity of written texts. This is not to suggest, of course, that factors such as the invention of printing and the resulting increased 'democratisation of knowledge' (Robinson 1999, pp246–249), have not had an impact on traditional practices of transmission and on the authority of those (the *'ulama*) traditionally deemed to be the carriers of knowledge.

In making a case for the reappraisal of the value of memorisation within contemporary Western education and culture, it is worth recalling Egan's point that there is an ambivalence towards the role of memorisation in contemporary Western society. For, as he rightly suggests, there is not only a general suspicion of memorisation as a learning tool but also, *at one and the same time*, a frequent condemnation in the popular press of contemporary methods for *not* teaching children 'basic facts', such as those connected with key events in British history. Within popular literature, too, writers often extol the fruits of childhood memorisation: as in this statement, for example: 'The schools I went to expected us to learn poems as homework, and I've never regretted anything I learned by heart when I was young' (Lumley 2004, p40).

In trying to make sense of these contradictions, it is useful to make a distinction between two terms that are often conflated in people's thinking: 'rote learning' and 'learning by heart.'[86] Reflection suggests that the role of the former, evoking as it does the sense of meaningless repetition, is limited—though still, perhaps, having a place in some circumstances and settings—whilst the latter is a far more meaningful exercise in which the memoriser's psyche and imagination—and, Boyle would suggest, physiology (Boyle 2004, eg pp 92, 115, 131)—are engaged and touched at a far deeper and more lasting level. If so, it would explain why rote learning is often the object of censure, not only in the Western tradition but in the Islamic too:

> Forced marriages and emphasis on the rote learning of Arabic, which lacks spontaneity and dynamic interpretation, are chasing some youngsters away from traditional religious instruction. (Malik 2004, p107; see also IBERR 2001, p6, and why the phrase 'learning a story by rote' sounds distinctly odd as compared to 'learning a story by heart'.)

It is memorisation of the latter kind that Egan undoubtedly extols when he links memory, imagination and learning. He suggests that a suspicion of memorisation is also rooted in the assumption that human memory is like that of a computer. He rejects any such static notion in that:

> [w]e are aware that our memory is neither like a static storehouse where data can be kept nor like a library where knowledge is stored in some coded form. Our memories are tied in with our emotions. Indeed, a better analogy for human memory might be the stomach: whatever goes in is transformed by its normal functioning. (Egan *op cit*)

It is in this much broader, richer sense that Boyle's affirms both memorisation in general as a distinct 'form of learning' (Boyle 2004, pp84–86) and Qur'anic memorisation in particular as a form of 'embodiment' (2.4). For, within the traditional Islamic culture of Morocco, she was able to detect a logic and coherence behind the practice of Qur'anic memorisation: that, if children memorise when they are young and their brains retentive, the value and beauty of what they have memorised can unfold itself during the rest of their lives:

> They can appreciate the beauty of words—the rhythm, the rhyme, the intonation (much as American children might be able to recite and enjoy nursery rhymes and poems or songs whose meanings are not actually clear to them). As the words of the Qur'an are engraved on the mind of the child, they can be retrieved, uncovered, and rediscovered. The meaning of the words unfolds itself over time, providing insights on how to live. (Boyle 2004, p92)

Thus, she posits:

> [the] embodied Qur'an acts as a point of reference, a compass, as children grow older, understand more of what they have memorised, and make decisions on the direction of their lives. (Boyle 2004, p131)

It must be borne in mind, however, that the Moroccan context in which Boyle carried out much of her fieldwork was one in which children would already have been familiar with the Arabic language. Her argument would undoubtedly lose much, though not all, of its power when transferred to a context, such as Britain, where Muslim children would be unfamiliar with Arabic as a language of discourse.

7.5 Barriers and pathways to development

The number of barriers that block the realisation of the ideal—Muslim supplementary education being a recognised component and participant in the larger educational community—are such that the ideal might seem an impossible one. There is, for example, the reluctance by both sides, Muslim and non-Muslim, to participate in such a venture with its implications of trust, openness and willingness to change.

From the Muslim side, such reluctance might stem from a range of sources, some of which—such as a mistrust of motives—are, no doubt, familiar to those researchers who have found their openings into British Muslim dar ul-uloom blocked (Gilliat-Ray 2005).

At the macro level, it might come also from a suspicion of the Western way of life and values, including the apparent raising of the intellectual above all other sources of knowledge: a suspicion that is part of what Buruma and Margalit (2004) have termed 'Occidentalism'. On the other hand, it might stem from a reluctance either to engage with civic action in general or with the ruling authorities in particular; traditional features of the Deobandi tradition, for instance (2.5; Geaves 1996, pp147–152).

There is also, no doubt, a range of barriers at the micro level, the kind that Martin et al identified as accounting for the lack of response from a number of Leicester 'complementary' schools (1.8) during their survey of 2004:

> The apparent reluctance to participate by some communities could stem from a lack of infrastructure that potentially supports such voluntary schools. Another possible reason is that schools might prefer to preserve their autonomy by remaining 'invisible', and may not see any potential advantages in sharing details of their organisational structures. (Martin et al 2004, p10)

From the non-Muslim side there might be barriers too. At the macro level, reluctance might stem from a general suspicion or fear of all things Islamic: the kind of approach that has come to be known as 'Islamophobia' (1.5). From the point of view of Western educators, it might also stem from a negative view of what takes place in mosque schools and an unwillingness to see what is regarded as mindless rote-learning, harsh discipline and excessive hours 'at the mosque' as worthy of the name of education at all. This might be exacerbated by what non-Muslims regard as 'unreasonableness' on the part of some Muslim educators: by insisting that non-Muslim visitors to a Muslim school wear Islamic-style clothing, for instance. A reluctance of mainstream educators to acknowledge the work of the 'private sector', an educational version of the traditional suspicion on the part of mainstream medical professionals of complementary and alternative medicine (CAM), might also be a factor.

But, at the same time, there are undoubtedly a number of current trends that would be conducive to the kind of symbiotic relationship that has been suggested in this study.

There is, for example, the growing interest in and use of networking in education, a process that intentionally sets out, as we have already seen (1.7), to bring together people from a range of settings in order, within conditions of growing trust, to engage in the sharing of experiences, knowledge-exchange and research. There is also the move at local authority level to break down traditional barriers between 'official' and 'voluntary' bodies (1.8) with a view to regarding the latter as a significant element and co-worker in the creation of community cohesion.[87]

Furthermore, there is the growing move from central government to encourage the emergent British Muslim community to address its own inner health and well-being so as to avoid the growth of the kind of extremist activity that led to the London bombings in July 2005. A good example of this was the setting up by the Home Office of seven working groups, under the banner 'Preventing Extremism Together', that each issued a report in October 2005. Within the recommendations of the working groups were a number that suggested an awareness of a growing need for conformity and regulation across Muslim supplementary education as well as for the latter to be seen as part of the wider educational community. For example, the Education Working Group's second recommendation was that the performance and achievement of Muslim pupils should be improved by strengthening a wide range of existing initiatives: through, for example:

> [p]romoting the use of the Extended Schools Programme to enhance and target the needs of Muslim parents (lifelong learning opportunities, families learning and parenting support programmes) and *build* (sic) *educational links with mosques and madrasahs*. (Home Office 2005, p25: stress added)

This working group also recommended that a British Muslim-led 'National Education Research and Foundation Centre be established', one of the activities of which could be:

> [r]esearching and developing curricular materials, particularly for interpersonal life-skills and citizenship to be used in maintained and independent schools *and madrasahs*. (Home Office 2005, p27: stress added)

For its part, the Imams/Mosques Working Group, which noted 'a huge potential for mosques as agents for the community, and social development' (Home Office 2005, p62), recommended '[t]he setting up of a National Resources Unit (NRU) for the development of curricula in madrasah/mosques and Islamic centres' (Home Office 2005, p63). Amongst other roles, it was suggested that the NRU could '[l]iaise with national and local education authorities to develop accredited educational modules that could be used in mainstream education subjects' (Home Office 2005, p66) and '[d]evelop best practice guidelines for mosques *and madrasahs*' (Home Office 2005, p66: stress added).

We have already noted (1.8) moves, at both local and national level, to set up organisations through which to acknowledge the contribution that supplementary schooling makes, to bring about a greater awareness of issues such as child protection, and to encourage contact across the supplementary/mainstream divide.

As well as these formal trends and developments, it is possible to point to specific examples of activity that indicate that some, Muslims and non-Muslims alike, are willing to leave traditional ways of thinking behind—including the failure to perceive any link between faith and non-faith educational activity—in order to create new patterns of relationship and working.

Take, for example, the research carried out by Ibrahim Lawson, on behalf of the National College for School Leadership (NCSL) and the Association of Muslim Schools (AMS), and which included a conference attended by headteachers of 35 UK-based Islamic schools (Lawson

2005a). Though this research was as much about the nature of leadership as that of Islamic Schools, its significance lies in a Muslim educationalist using the apparatus of mainstream education, as embodied in the National College for School Leadership, to foster improvement within the Muslim educational sector. Moreover, in that the intention of the research was to 'hold up a mirror to this world [the Islamic schooling community] in order for the schools themselves *and those outside the Muslim community* to see more clearly what is happening, what the leadership issues might be and where the future lies' (Lawson 2005b: stress added) it was seen by Lawson as having implications for all educators, regardless of their background or faith commitment.

Again, there are the actions by individuals or groups who see a need and, of their own volition, act upon it. One example is that of Freda Hussain, headteacher of Moat Community College in Leicester: that is, a Muslim headteacher of a mainstream local authority secondary school (TES 2005). Under the auspices of the Leicester Complementary Schools Trust (1.8), links were established between her own school and local mosques and their supplementary classes so that both they and the school might benefit (Personal visit, June 2005).

Another example was the professional link, under the auspices of Manchester's Diversity and Inclusion Team support of supplementary schools (2.7), established between Madrassa Talim-ul-Islam School and Cheetham CE Community Primary School. Though, 'traditionally and historically' the main focus of the former was to 'provide cultural and religious education':

> [t]he school management has perceived a need to find the means to enhance the learning experience of the children and to update its teaching methods. In order to meet this objective they intend to utilise their existing strong links with Cheetham CE Community Primary School. The volunteer teachers are currently involved in a training initiative lead by the mainstream school. The first phase of this initiative has been completed. Mainstream teachers have visited and observed classes in

the Supplementary School. They have reported on their findings. The teachers at the Madrassa will be involved in adapting and modifying their teaching strategies to incorporate current mainstream techniques. This will be carried out on an on-going basis with visits to the mainstream school to observe literacy lessons. (Manchester City Council 2005)

What is lacking from this ground-breaking venture, of course, is any suggestion that mainstream teachers, too, could gain from this exercise.

Though the suggestion that there would be gains from Muslim supplementary classes being seen as a partner within the wider educational community is central to this thesis, a number of other suggestions have also been made. In the final chapter, which will also include a series of recommendations, these suggestions will be brought together and placed in context.

8
Overview, Conclusions and Recommendations

8.1 Introduction

In chapters 1 to 7, the outcomes of ethnographic fieldwork within one Redbridge Muslim community have been presented and placed within a range of contexts: historical, cultural, biographical, religious, educational and academic. The purpose of this final chapter is, through presenting an overview (8.2), to draw a number of conclusions some of which represent developments or refinements of ideas that have already been introduced. There then follow ten recommendations (8.3) that, for clarity, have been grouped under three headings.

8.2 Overview and conclusions

There is an increasingly strong Muslim presence both within Europe in general and Britain in particular. Though Muslim stereotypes which suggest Islamophobic prejudice are always likely to surface, there is also evidence of an increasingly serious engagement with the nature, role and evolution of the British Muslim population (1.5).

Muslim Supplementary Classes

Given the key position of knowledge, education and learning within Islam (2.2), educational provision has been a feature of the British Muslim community since its earliest days. As the community—or, more accurately 'communities'—became established, such provision has become both more diverse and more organised (2.6).

A significant part of this educational provision has been that provided for young Muslims, usually, but not always, associated with local mosques. There is now a considerable number of supplementary classes, often referred to as maktabs, attached to mosques. Because there is no overall system of regulation or registration, it is impossible to know either how many maktabs exist or the number of children who attend them (5.1). It is safe to assert, however, that tens of thousands of young British Muslims spend many hours each week at such institutions. For these children, and the extended families to which they belong, their experience at mosque supplementary classes forms a significant element in their overall experience of life.

The form of education that is found within British Muslim supplementary classes, as in institutions of higher Islamic learning, has been affected profoundly by traditional patterns of Islamic education (2.3). This is most obvious in the emphasis on Qur'anic memorisation (2.4). Rather than being a relic of pre or proto literate cultural settings, however, Qur'anic memorisation is rooted in beliefs about how the sounds of the Qur'an were revealed, heard and transmitted. As such, the traditional Western perception of the Qur'an as a *book* does not do full justice to the Muslim perception of the Qur'an as a profound oral-aural experience in which word and sound are indivisible. Another traditional feature of Islamic education is the use of the learning circle (halaqa: 2.3, 5.4) in which the teacher can coach individuals on a one-to-one basis—the dominant method—but also work with the whole group or small groups.

British educational practice, however, has also been affected heavily by everyday practice in the homelands, notably the Indian sub-continent, of Muslim immigrants to Britain. Thus, for example, the language of discourse in mosque classes, particularly in the early days of the British Muslim community, was that spoken by the first generation of immigrants (Urdu and Gujarati, for example) and discipline often relied heavily on physical methods. Teachers who were brought over from lands of origin by British mosque committees have often perpetuated both non-English communication and the use of corporal punishment. Furthermore, they have often had little understanding of the culture and world of young British Muslims. Many members of the British Muslim community have voiced concerns over the negative impact of this (1.6).

As the British Muslim community has grown in size and an increasing number are British-born, there is evidence of change in the provision of supplementary education. It is in this respect that the focus of the fieldwork outlined in this study—the supplementary classes held at Balfour Road Mosque in Redbridge (chapters 5–6)—is of such significance. Here, where an increasingly large number of the teachers are British-born and British-trained, the predominant language of discourse is now English. Though learning to read and memorise the Qur'an remains the core activity, and exceptionally able students can join hifz classes in order to memorise the entire Qur'an (chapter 6), learning is structured and sequenced through the use of South African-produced curriculum material (5.5). Training is provided for teachers and the use of corporal punishment is not permitted. High standards of personal appearance are insisted upon. Practices that are found in mainstream local authority schools, such as the issuing of reports on students, are used increasingly. Moreover, and largely though the influence of one of the British-born but Deobandi-influenced imams who has served as mosque school principal, the committee and teachers have shown themselves willing to discuss their practices and, in the case of this study, to be a focus of ethnographic research. Thus, to use Boyle's phrase, maktabs can serve as 'agents' of both 'preservation and change' (Boyle 2004).

Though Qur'anic memorisation remains a central feature of traditional Muslim learning, and the practices of the Prophet Muhammad have had a profound effect on the tradition of teaching and learning (2.2), there is nothing in principle to prevent Muslim educators drawing from the range of pedagogical techniques that are currently available. The prohibition against innovation (*bid'a*) applies to belief rather than practice (interview with Muslim scholar, Cambridge, January 2003). Where a halt would be called for would be if questioning was allowed, free-rein, to challenge the basis on which Muslim belief itself stands (Halstead 1995).

Overall, little is known outside the Muslim community of the rationale, structure and practice of mosque supplementary classes. There is a remarkable dearth of ethnographic-based material (2.3, 2.6). What literature there is about Muslim educational life in Britain tends to focus on mainstream schooling, particularly the attempt by some Muslim groups to gain voluntary-aided status for the Muslim schools that they represent (2.6). Many non-Muslim teachers in mainstream schools retain stereotyped and negative views of Muslim supplementary classes, not only as institutions (which demand many hours of Muslim children's attendance above and beyond time spent at 'day' school) but also of what takes place in them; as places where there is both excessive rote learning, with little understanding on the part of the children, and excessive use of physical methods to discipline them. The quality of what takes place within such classes is also contested, however, within the Muslim community itself and influences the decision by some families to employ tutors or to teach their children themselves (4.2, 4.7).

There are undoubtedly many issues that need addressing in British Muslim supplementary classes. These include an undue emphasis on rote learning at the expense of understanding, the training provided for teachers, the methods used to maintain control and concentration, and issues related to health and safety, including child protection.

Nevertheless, as the research into the world and work of one hifz class demonstrated (chapter 6), supplementary classes can appear to have remarkable success in fostering personal piety and commitment in their students, and in supporting that tenacity that leads to an extraordinary intellectual achievement: the commitment to memory of the entire Qur'an in Arabic. But, as we have seen, this is not a solitary achievement on the part of students for they are supported by the entire community amongst which what they learn and gain is valued greatly. The metaphor of 'capital', combined with a range of terms such as 'cultural' and 'spiritual', is helpful in articulating and understanding the personal and communal value of what students gain from involvement in supplementary classes (7.2). Though there are already references to 'social capital' in existing literature about Islamic education, this study has extended the use of the capital metaphor through using a range of qualifiers. Amongst other things, this exercise suggested that the capital that students accrue as a result of supplementary mosque education might be of benefit not only to themselves and the Muslim community of which they are members but also to society as a whole.

There are signs within the British Muslim community of a growing demand that some kind of national structure is needed in which to develop and disseminate best practice amongst mosque schools, including curricula and issues related to child protection (7.5). Given the very loose and diverse nature of the British Muslim community, however, it is impossible at this stage to know what the outcome of this demand will be.

In the mean time, a number of local authorities have set up organisations through which to provide support for supplementary classes, Muslim and non-Muslim, and to encourage sharing and cooperation between them (1.8). Through such organisations, a growing range of material is being gathered about supplementary schooling in general. This study adds to that general stock.

There are also instances, like those featured in this study (7.3, 7.5), where individuals have sought to create the conditions in which Muslim supplementary classes, as part of the wider educational community, can both contribute to and gain from educational discussion and discourse.

Such instances resonate with the increased interest in and use of networking within the mainstream educational sector (1.7) and also with the recognition, at local government level, that voluntary organisations have much to contribute towards community cohesion (1.8).

If, rather than as a little known and understood feature of Muslim community life, supplementary classes are seen as part of the wider educational community, the conjecture in this study is that there could be gains both for these classes and for mainstream schooling. Such benefits can be represented as a spectrum, from the small- to the large-scale. Examples of small-scale interaction are the sharing of information about what educational resources are available or when examinations and tests are to be held at either institution. More significant interaction would be the sharing of resources, such as ICT facilities, and acknowledgement in mainstream school of educational achievements associated with supplementary classes: having memorised portions of the Qur'an, having completed its reading or, indeed, memorised it in entirety. At the more subtle and fuller end of the spectrum, there could be joint observation and discussion between teachers about pedagogy—including the role of memorisation, as distinct from rote learning (7.5)—and how best to discipline, motivate and engage children of today (Mogra 2004). As this study has shown, there have already been small-scale activities and experiments that suggest that, given the right conditions, such things are possible.

But, at a more profound level still is the suggestion that such interaction is not simply an attempt by the mainstream school sector to bring Muslim supplementary classes 'up to scratch': indeed, such a one-sided position would be redolent of the situation in many colonised cultures where schools run on colonial models were characterised as both 'modern' and 'advanced', to the detriment of traditional styles of schooling (2.3).[88] By contrast, the conjecture here is that both Muslim supplementary classes and British mainstream schools represent different educational traditions, each with its own educational philosophy and ways of thinking, practical outworking, strengths and weaknesses. For, if Muslim supplementary classes can be characterised as archaic, indoctrinatory and physical, then mainstream local authority schools could be characterised as institutions which are dominated by the novel (the new), the rational, and achievement that can be measured in numerical terms. By contrast, each tradition also has its strengths. In terms of the maktab tradition, these would include: the high value placed on knowledge and learning, the close bond between student and teacher, the high regard for the teacher as a purveyor of knowledge, the use of memorisation as a distinct form of learning, the intellectual being placed within the context of a range of types of development (2.2), and the emphasis on each child doing his or her best irrespective of how others are doing.

As such, encounter between representatives of the two traditions—given the right conditions of time, trust and openness—could bring benefit to both. Ultimately, of course, the beneficiaries would not only be the teachers that represent each tradition, but the children with whom they work and, for whom, 'Muslim' might be only one facet of their multiple identities (1.3: Baumann 1996). If many Muslims are searching for ways in which not only Islam but also British society can be rejuvenated, what better way could there be than this?

8.3 Areas for future research

- Research into the nature of supplementary Muslim schooling in Britain so as to identify, for instance, different practices and styles (eg between Barelvi- and Deobandi-orientated provision) and evidence of: change over time, curriculum innovation and experimentation, and collaborative work within the wider educational and social community.
- Research into the impact of mosque supplementary schooling on the lives of Muslim children in general, and on their learning potential in mainstream schooling in particular. This could be achieved through a variety of ethnographic methods such as

observation of Muslim students in both settings (ie maktab and mainstream school) and the carrying out of semi-structured interviews (with students, family members and teachers).

- Research into memorisation as a distinct and legitimate form of learning, within both Muslim and non-Muslim settings. This could include analysis of the terms 'memorisation', 'rote learning' and 'learning by heart' as well as identification of examples of where memorisation is already part of Western, non-Muslim culture, though perhaps not identified as such.
- Research into the role of British imams so as to identify, for example: their changing cultural, linguistic and educational backgrounds; their involvement in Muslim supplementary education; their role within the wider community, Muslim and non-Muslim.
- Research into the role and significance of the hafiz within the British Muslim community in order not only to identify the more direct ways in which their recitation skills are utilised (eg during Ramadan Tarawih prayers) but also within the wider life of the Muslim community and beyond.

8.4 Recommendations

Recommendations relating to methods and material used in religious education

- That, in order to counteract the tendency to treat the Qur'an as a written text, classroom practice in religious education includes imaginative ways of presenting the Qur'an as an oral/aural experience in the lives of Muslims. This would certainly include providing the opportunity for students to *hear* the Qur'an.[89]
- That, following the lead given by Jackson, Nesbitt, Smalley (eg 2005) and others, not only is ethnographic material relating to the lives and traditions of British Muslims used as a significant resource to be investigated and interpreted by students, but

that ethnographic methods themselves are used by students in gathering material.

Recommendations for the work of maktabs, mainstream schools and local authorities

- That mainstream schools with Muslim pupils take a positive interest in the experiences of these students in supplementary classes and, when appropriate, recognise their learning achievements there (eg in having read the whole Qur'an, or committed substantial sections to memory).
- That maktabs liaise with mainstream schools and vice versa in order to find out how each institution can aid the work of the other.
- That local authorities, drawing from the experience accrued in such authorities as Birmingham, Kirklees, Leicester and Manchester, consider whether they have the capacity to set up structures in order to promote cross-fertilisation of ideas and methods across mosque supplementary classes, between these classes and other forms of supplementary schooling, and between these classes and mainstream schooling.

Glossary of Non-English Terms Used in the Text

A brief note on the root base of Arabic words and transliterating them into English. For those who (like me) are not Arabic speakers or readers, it might be useful to be reminded that:
1. Arabic words are generally based on a 'root' of three consonants which shape the underlying meaning/s of a word. To take three examples:
    • the root S-L-M connotes meanings of 'being safe', 'to surrender', 'to submit'. Thus: the word iSLaM relates to the relationship of total submission to Allah, the word muSLiM relates to a person who has submitted him or herself to Allah; the word SaLaaM, as in the everyday greeting 'peace be upon you', is also connected to the same root meaning 'peace'.
    • the root K-T-B connotes meanings of 'marking', inscribing' or 'writing'. Thus, the word KiTaB means 'book', the word KaTiB' means 'writer', and the word 'maKTaB' refers to a place of elementary study (and also to a desk, literally meaning 'place of study').

- the root H-F-Z connotes meanings of 'securing', 'protecting', 'taking care of', 'preserving' and 'saving'. Thus, the process of memorising and thus preserving and protecting the words and sound of the Arabic Qur'an, is called 'HiFZ', and the person who has achieved this either a 'HaFiZ' (male) or 'HaFiZa' (female). The plural form is HuFfaZ.

2. In that the Arabic and Roman alphabets belong to very different traditions (the former to the Semitic), there are often many variant spellings of an Arabic word in Roman script. In the following list of Arabic words used in this book, with occasional reference to other cognate words used in languages like Urdu, some of the most common variant spellings of particular words are also cited.

For simplicity, diacritical marks have been omitted.

Adab/Aadaab	This subtle word, often twinned with akhlaq, has a wide range of meanings such as 'proper deportment', 'good manners', 'ideal behaviour' and 'erudition'.
Akhlaaq/Akhlaq	'Morals', a person's 'ethical code'.
Alim	A scholar, a person learned in religion and law, a graduate of a madrasa. Note the link with 'ilm ('knowledge').
Allah	The Arabic word for 'God' which is incapable, grammatically, of being put into the plural form. Arabic-speaking Christians also use this term.
Barelvi	Relating to a Muslim movement, founded in Bareilly in India by Maulana Ahmad Raza Khan (1856-1921), that gives a particularly high respect to the person of the Prophet Muhammad as a model and inspiration for Muslim life. Pirs (spiritual guides) and customs around shrines are highly venerated in this tradition. Within

Glossary of Non-English Terms Used in the Text

	forms of Islam of South East Asian origins, Barelvis are often contrasted with Deobandis.
Bismillah al Rahman al Rahim	The Muslim blessing (usually referred to as 'The Basmala'), meaning 'In the Name of God, the Compassionate, the Merciful', which begins all but one surah/chapter (the ninth) of the Qur'an.
Dar ul-uloom/Dar al-ulum	Literally, a 'house of learning', an Islamic college of higher studies such as Arabic and jurisprudence.
Deobandi	Relating to a Muslim movement founded in India in 1867 and named after an Islamic seminary called Darul Uloom Deoband, situated 90 miles from Delhi. The movement is often regarded as fairly 'puritan' in approach in rejecting many of the traditions – such as the veneration of pirs and customs around shrines – associated with the Barelvis.
Dhor	'Revision', an Urdu word often used by those undertaking hifz. (The Arabic equivalent is muraja'ah).
Fajr	The first of the five times of daily set prayer at dawn.
Fitra	A subtle term that refers to the intrinsic, pure nature of human beings into which they are born and which 'contains the blueprint of the original form of the divine law' (Geaves, 2006, p33).
Hadith	A traditional report of something that the Prophet Muhammad did, said, or approved of. This, together with the Qur'an, forms the basis of Islamic law and practice (sunna).
Hafiz	A male who has committed the whole of the Arabic Qur'an to memory.
Hafiza	A female who has committed the whole of the Arabic Qur'an to memory.

Muslim Supplementary Classes

Halaqa/ Halaka/ Halqa	Literally, a 'loop' or 'circle'. Refers to a learning circle, that is, a circle of Halaka, Halqa students who gather in front of a teacher, a practice that goes back to the time of the Prophet. By extension, it can refer to any group of Muslims that meet for study or discussion - a 'woman's learning circle', for instance.
Hifz	The process of committing the words and sound of the Arabic Qur'an to memory.
Hijab	The headscarf worn by many Muslim women.
Ilm	The Arabic term for 'knowledge' which is said to be the third most common word to be found in the Qur'an. See also related words such as alim and ulama.
Imam	'Faith', the quality of the believer.
Iman/ Imaan	In the majority, Sunni form of Islam, the person who leads prayer and who will therefore stand at the front of any gathering meeting for prayer. As a title, the word has particular significance for Shi'a Muslims.
Insaan	The Urdu and Arabic word for 'human being'. The word is sometimes used, particularly by Muslims of a Sufi persuasion, in a qualitative sense to mean a real human being.
Isnad	The chain of transmission – of a hadith, for instance.
Jubba	Long, plain tunic, covering the body from the neck to the ankles, worn by some Muslim girls and women
Juz	The word literally means 'part' or 'particle' and is used to refer to a thirtieth part of the Qur'an. The last juz – the one containing the shortest surahs which young Muslims usually commit to memory first of all – is known as 'Juz Amma' (surahs 78-114). Muslims who originate from south-east Asia often use the Urdu term sipara, sometimes shortened to para.

Glossary of Non-English Terms Used in the Text

Kalimah	The first of the five 'pillars' of Islam, the declaration of faith, la illaha illa Allah, Muhammad rasul Allah, meaning 'There is no god but God; and Muhammad is the Messenger of God'.
Khalifah	An Arabic term that is used to refer to humans beings as the vicegerents of Allah on Earth. In Sunni Islam, this term is used for the Caliphs or the successors of the Prophet Muhammad.
Khatm-e-Qur'an/ Khatm al-Qur'an	Literally, a 'completion' or 'sealing' of the Qur'an and which refers to the completion of the reading/recitation of the whole Qur'an, either simultaneously by a group of Muslims or by an individual over a period of time. The former practice is often carried out to mark a special event such as a funeral.
Kitab	An Arabic word, found 260 times in the Qur'an, that refers to anything that is written or noted down. For Muslims, the supreme and unchanging Kitab is the Qur'an.
Loh/Lawh	An Arabic word sometimes used for the wooden board that has been traditionally used to learn Arabic writing and the words of the Qur'ān in some north African countries (Libya, for example).
Madrasah/ Madrassah	A word, derived from the Arabic root D-R-S connoting 'to study', that is used with various shades of meaning to mean a place of Muslim learning but is often used to refer to an institution of higher Muslim learning.
Maktab	The title given in some Muslim communities to the elementary school to which children go to begin their basic Muslim studies such as learning the Arabic alphabet and how to decode Arabic words. Maktabs are often mosque-based.

Malvi/ Mulvi	A title, literally meaning 'my master' in Arabic, sometimes used of a Muslim religious teacher in the Indo-Pakistani subcontinent. The kindred term maulana means 'our master'. It is often used with the reverential suffix Saheb (or Saab). Thus, a religious teacher is described or addressed as Maulvi Saab or Maulana Saheb. As a direct address, pupils will call their teachers Shaykh, Ustadh or Huzoor.
Namaz	The Urdu word for the Arabic salah/salat meaning set prayer: that which is performed five times daily.
Niyyah/Niyya	'Intention': in Islam, any religious act (such as performing ablutions before set prayer) must be preceded with conscious intent so as to prevent it becoming an automatic and empty gesture.
Sabaq	Literally 'lesson', the Urdu word used in some cultures for the new portion of the Qur'an that someone undertaking hifz is about to memorise. The Arabic equivalent is dars.
Salah *Salaat*	The second of the five 'pillars' of Islam, the performance of set prayers Salat, five times daily.
Sawab	Religious benefit or merit accruing, for example, from recitation of the Qur'an or convening a khatm-e-Qur'an.
Sipara	The Urdu word, sometimes shortened to para, which refers to a thirtieth portion of the Qur'an. The Arabic equivalent is juz'.
Surah/Sura	The 114 chapters into which the written text of the Qur'an is divided. Each surah has a traditional title relating on a key word or theme within it.
Surah Yasin/Surah Yaseen	Surah 36, considered to be the 'heart of the Qur'an'. It is often recited in front of those who are on the deathbed or those who have died.

Glossary of Non-English Terms Used in the Text

Surat al-Fatihah	The 'Opener', the traditional title of surah 1 of the Qur'an. A pious Muslim, who completes his or her five set prayers each day, recites the Fatihah at least 17 times daily.
Tablighi Jama'at	An organisation – the so-called 'preaching party' – founded in the late 1920s and whose mission is to bring back Muslims to a full commitment to Islam. Its European headquarters is located at the Deobandi Dar ul-uloom in Dewsbury, West Yorkshire.
Ta'lim/Ta'leem	'Instruction', often stated as being one – together with tarbiyyah and ta'dib of the three key elements of Muslim education.
Tarawih/Taraweeh	Special cycle of late evening prayers that take place over the course of the month of Ramadan and during which, cumulatively, the whole Qur'an is recited by one or more Hafiz.
Tarbiyah/Tarbiya	Nurturing in order to build character, often cited as one of the three key elements, if not the main element, of Islamic education.
Ta'dib	The systems of rules and regulations that regulate the correct oral rendering of the Qur'an: for example, nasal sounds, elongation of long vowels to varying degrees, and articulation of sounds from different parts of the mouth.
Tajwid	The systems of rules and regulations that regulate the correct oral rendering of the Qur'an: for example, nasal sounds, elongation of long vowels to varying degrees, and articulation of sounds from different parts of the mouth.
Tawhid	'Oneness', the Unity of God

Muslim Supplementary Classes

Thaub/Thawb/ Thobe	A full-length garment, often plain white, worn by men in some Muslim communities. Also sometimes called a jubba/jubbah.
Topi	A word often used to refer to the prayer cap worn by some Muslim men.
Ulama	The plural form of alim (learned person, scholar); thus, Muslim religious scholars and clerics.
Umma/Ummah	The world-wide body of Muslims of which the individual Muslim is a part.
Ustaad/Ustaadh	The word for teacher in Arabic is Ustaadh (ending with a light z sound) whereas its equivalent in Urdu is Ustaad (ending with a d).
Yakeen/Yaqeen	Certainty, firm belief. A higher level of belief based on conviction.

Endnotes and Commentary

1   Since the writing of this thesis, a number of further studies on Islam within Britain have been written, including: *Young, British and Muslim* by Philip Lewis (2007), Muslims in Britain by Sophie Gilliat-Ray (2010), and *Muslims in Scotland: The Making of Community in a Post-9/11 World* by Stefano Bonino (2017).

2   Note: Scourfield et al (2013, p8): 'it is difficult to speak about a 'Muslim community' in Britain. Instead, it is better to regard British Muslims as part of diverse linguistic, ethnic, racial, and geographically dispersed communities that retain strong transnational kinship links around the globe, as well as an abiding sense of identification with the worldwide Muslim population (the Ummah)'.

3   Compare: 'Great ethnic and theological diversity can be found in British Muslim communities. In fact, there are communities within communities, each containing a multitude of different talents and needs' and 'The Muslim presence in Britain is not a singular presence, and it is important to hold this diversity constantly in mind' (Suleiman et al, 2009, p9, p16).

4   There is a fascinating passing reference to chain migration and to what came to be known as 'the myth of return' at the very beginning of a film, based on ethnographic interviews with members of the Muslim community in Yorkshire of Indian/Pakistani heritage: 'From Parks to Pavilions: Documenting the History of Asian Cricket in Yorkshire' (2016), https://youtu.be/g7ybi54L3mc

5   The figures referred to here have, of course, been superseded by those emanating from the 2011 census. Amongst other statistics, the latter showed that the population of Muslims in England and Wales had risen from 1.55 million in 2001 to 2.71 million in 2011.

6   Because of the holding of the 2011 national census since the writing of the original text, the figures given in this section are now clearly out of date. The 2011 census data, for instance, showed that the total Redbridge population had risen to 278.970 by 2011, the proportion of Muslims increasingly very significantly from 11.9% in 2001 to 23.3% in 2011.

7   And, at that time, the sixth largest Muslim population of the 33 London boroughs.

8   This statement is no longer true as there is now a Shi'a community centre—the 'Muslim Community of Essex'—which was founded in 2010 in the Newbury Park area of Redbridge and which, amongst other facilities, offers a 'madrassah' on weekdays as well as on Saturday and Sunday (www.ic-e.org/).

9   See also Geaves (2010).

10 The College no longer exists under this title.

11 This government department has reverted back to a simpler title—the Department for Education (DfE).

12 The current National Resource Centre for Supplementary Education (https:/www.supplementaryeducation.org.uk/), a registered charity, was formed in 2006.

13 With hindsight, more could have been said in this section about a distinctive feature of Islamic education, namely, 'the personalisation of knowledge': the essential link between teacher and taught in the process of the transmission of knowledge. Of one late medieval site of Islamic learning, Cairo, for example, it has been said that 'education... rested on an informal system of personal relationships rather than institutional reputation and affiliation' (Berkey 1992, p85). Note, also, Abdullah Sahin's comment on his own experience as a young person in a Turkish *imam hatit* (state-organised special religious school). Though modelled on a secular western model: 'it ... included memorisation & repetition,

and was text-&-teacher centred. The only difference between these schools & madrasah was that the madrasah system was organised as an organic extension of the mosque and its religious culture. Therefore, it had a real experiential dimension that created intimacy and trust between the teacher and the student'. (Sahin 2013, 19; my italics). See also, Makdisi (1981) and Chamberlain (1994).

14 It is interesting (and perhaps slightly controversial) that Tariq Ramadan (2008, p40 *& passim*) translates the Arabic word *Rabb* as 'Educator'.

15 See also Rosenthal (2007), 20. It was Franz Rosenthal who, in his classic work Knowledge Triumphant: The Concept of Knowledge in Medieval Islam, claimed that reverence for knowledge ('ilm) was to become 'the main theme of Islamic civilisation' (p18) and that 'There is no branch of Muslim intellectual life, of Muslim religious and political life, and of the daily life of the average Muslim that remained untouched by the all-pervasive attitude toward 'knowledge' as something of supreme value for Muslim being. 'Ilm is Islam …' (p2).

16 Note also, Al-Ghazali's advice to students: 'The student's immediate purpose should be the attainment of inner virtue, and his ultimate goal should be to draw close to God and achieve spiritual perfection rather than to gain authority and to look impressive in front of his peers': *The Revival of the Sciences of Religion*, cited by Günther (2006), p384.

17 See also: Ramadan (2008), pp102–103. Mattson (2008), p88 refers to the use of the phrase 'That is sufficient' by Qur'anic teachers in imitation of Muhammad's own words in order to make it clear that a student has recited enough of the Qur'an at that particular sitting.

18 *Tarbiya* is a key concept in the current work of Abdullah Sahin (eg 2013) in formulating a thorough critical rationale for contemporary Islamic pedagogy and identity formation.

19 Compare: 'Islamic education is concerned not only with the transmission of knowledge (*ta'lim*) but also with the education of the whole being and development of human character (*tarbiyyah*)', Suleiman et al (2009), p68.

20 Also see Makdisi (1981) and Berkey (1992).

21 Though some historical autobiographical material can be both fascinating and useful in showing the actual lived experience of children and young people in mosque-based and other forms of Islamic education across different cultures and time periods. See, for example, Hussein (1981) and Qutb (2004).

22 Note: 'Qur'anic recitation is both an art form and a form of worship in the Muslim world', GLA/Mayor of London (2006, p79)

23 This hypothesis—that the west has increasingly privileged the visual at the expense of the aural—has been taken up by Charles Hirschkind: see, in particular, Hirschkind 2006, pp13–14. This is one of the reasons, he suggests, why nineteenth western travellers to the east regarded the Arabic language as over-embellished and discordant. This is beautifully illustrated in the following account of the activities taking place in a 'medressy' (sic) in Alexandria recorded in his travelogue by the nineteenth century British traveller and author, James Augustus St John (1795–1875): 'While studying, or rather learning to repeat, their lessons, each boy declaims his portion of the Koran aloud at the same time, rocking his body to and fro, in order, according to their theory, to assist his memory; and as every one seemed desirous of drowning the voices of his companions, the din produced by so many shrill discordant notes reminds one of the 'labourers of Babel' (St John, 1845, pp31–32).

24 Note: 'With every new revelation, the Prophet would recite the new addition to the Qur'an to those around him, who would eagerly learn it and in turn recite it to others', Abdel Haleem (2004) pxv.

25 Note: 'In reciting the Qur'an, the very words of God are reproduced in the throats of the reciters and perceived in the ears and minds of listeners. With each articulation of a Qur'anic phrase, the believer is recreating speech of a God who is as alive today as he has been forever. This is not a performance of historical speech but a rearticulation of the eternal words of the living God', Mattson (2008), p82.

26 Note: an *isnad* (certificate) only refers to people/reciters, not to a book: see Mattson (2008), p83.

27 Note: 'It is only through oral teaching that all aspects of *tajwid*, as well as more subtle qualities of recitation such as pitch and tempo, can be transmitted', Mattson (2008), p85.

28 In the whole area of the reception of sound and the development of the human sensorium, with particular reference to Muslim culture and soundscape, the work of Charles Hirschkind (2001, 2004, 2006) makes for fascinating reading. (See also note 24 above.)

29 See also Mattson (2008), p32: 'What is impossible to convey when translating these verses [ie of the Qur'an] is the way their sound when recited accords so well with their meaning. Perhaps it is not even enough to say that the sound of the recitation is in harmony with the meaning of the words, but that the sound itself conveys meaning'.

30 A different but equally evocative experience is recalled by Michael Sells with reference to the extraordinary impact of a bus driver playing a cassette of Qur'anic recitation on an over-crowded bus traveling to Alexandria (2009, pp183–184).

31 The concept of 'embodiment' is highly significant within Muslim thinking and hermeneutics. See, for example, the title of Rudolf T Ware III's book (2014): *The Walking Qur'an: Islamic Education, Embodied Knowledge, and History in West Africa*. See, also, Gent 2018 (in press).

32 This lacuna has been partially filled by ongoing research carried out by the author: see, for example, Gent (2016).

33 For the titles of some of the key books on Britain in the United Kingdom published since this study, see note 1 above.

34 We are here entering, of course, the territory of types of activity that some Muslims might object to on the grounds of practice being more about superstition and folk-belief than 'genuine religion'. Novels involving everyday life in Muslims communities are often a rich source for finding out about such practice. Take, for example, an episode described in K Hosseini's novel *The Kite Runner* (2003): 'They piled their things in the centre of a few worn rags and tied the corners together. We loaded the bundle into the Buick. Hassan stood in the threshold of the house and held the Koran as we all kissed it and passed under it. Then we left for Kabul' (p182). A similar ritual is also described in the same author's later novel, *A Thousand Splendid Suns* (2007, p347).

35 Note Coles (2008), p33: 'Given that the majority of British Muslim youth are likely to attend madrasahs until they are at least fourteen, there is surprisingly little material available for well researched comment'.

36 Some attempts at estimating the number of Muslim children who attend supplementary classes has been attempted, however. According to Cherti & Bradley (2011, p3), for example, there are about 2000 'madrassas' operating in Britain attended by about 250,000 Muslim children.

37 See, also, Berglund (2010), p48, for references to the challenges that she faced as a researcher in trying to make contact with Muslim schools in Sweden.

38 Geaves (2007, pp1–2) gives a useful definition of reflexivity: 'Reflexivity is an anthropological term used to describe the role of scholars in the research process and their self-conscious location of themselves in their research … Reflexivity is defined as the process of bending one's own experience back on one's self or, alternatively, being conscious of ourselves as we see ourselves'. Knott (2009, p19), on the other hand, is more concise: 'the ability to be self-aware and knowledgeable about where we stand in relation to the subjects we write about and to use this awareness constructively'.

39 In fact, Erricker (2001, p159) comments on Kvale's metaphors of the qualitative research interviewer as a miner or traveller.

40 See also, Gent (2006).

41 For accounts of various kinds of recitation competition held in Indonesia in the last decade of the twentieth century, see Rasmussen (2001) (2010). See also the HBO documentary, *Koran by Heart*, directed by Greg Barker, about a major international Qur'an recitation competition held in Cairo in 2010: https://www.youtube.com/watch?v=ptHdmw57rzM

42 There are many references to corporal punishment in the range of literature—academic as well as popular (such as autobiographies and novels)—that touches on traditional Muslim education (as, presumably, there are in parallel literature relating to other educational traditions). See, for example: Eickelman (1978) pp493–4; Nofal (1993), p6; Boyle (2006), p284; Al Raee (2009), pp26–27; Alam (2011), p171f; Sardar (2011), ch1; Sarwar (2016), p53.

43 For more about the role of the hafiz within the Muslim community, see Gent 2016.

44 In an article carried by *The Times* in December 2008, it was stated that there are almost 1600 madrassas in Britain involving c200,000 children. Coles (2008) conjectured that, 'It is estimated that the majority of those aged 4 to 14 attend madrassahs after school' (p6). Also, see note 37 above.

45 These plans have come to fruition. The main mosque building is now significantly larger than it was when this comment was originally written, offering better classroom facilities amongst other things. See section on 'Masjid Renovation Project' on the mosque website: www.ilfordMuslimsociety.org/

46 By 2017, as we would expect, things have moved on. The maktab has a principal, it now serves an agreed catchment area, there are over 350 students together with a waiting list, there are over 20 teachers, and administration is computer-based and served by a volunteer administrative team.

47 It is an easy mistake for newcomers to this field to think that a British Muslim whose heritage lies in the Gujarat implied that family members emigrated straight from the Gujarat to Britain. In fact, for many such people, the move was to parts of Africa (like Kenya or Uganda) first and then, later, with changed circumstances, to Britain. This can lead to some strange juxtapositions—as, for example, at the current time (2017), the reference to 'Bengali-Italians'.

48 A great deal of research has been carried out in the field of Literacy Studies on the phenomenon of 'language shift'—the gradual change from one home language to another (eg from Urdu or Mirpuri-Panjabi to English): see, for example, Rosowsky (2010).

49 See Abdullah Sahin's comment about his own experience as a young person in a Turkish *imam hatit* (state-organised special religious school). Though modelled on a secular western model: 'it ... included memorisation and repetition, and was text-and-teacher centred. The only difference between these schools and *madrasah* was that the *madrasah* system was organised as an organic extension of the mosque and its religious culture. Therefore, *it had a real experiential dimension that created intimacy and trust between the teacher and the student*' (Sahin 2013, 19; my italics).

50 There is a delightful piece of observational language, extracted from field notes gathered in autumn 2014, concerning the sound of a mosque worship hall being used for supplementary education by Andrey Rosowsky's (2016, p139): 'There is the pleasant "hum" of recitation going on in the main prayer hall. Some really beautiful voices can be heard from this general "hum". I am tempted to record what I can hear but I haven't asked permission for this so refrain from doing so. I try to describe it in words. There are different sounds and timbres, varying volumes and pitches, of adolescent voices: some are high, some unbroken, some broken, punctuated now and then by the deeper baritone voice of the male teacher. Some boys recite very quietly (almost silently) whilst other voices dominate. Today I am really taken by the sound as it passes around the prayer hall. It has its ebbs and flows—or is like the wind. It eases then starts up again for no outward reason—no reminders from the teacher or anyone else. There is a sense of a pause which is shared by all who then seem to sense how long it should last. One boy starts to recite again—the teacher is busy with a student at the front. But the other boys all start again for no obvious reason—a subconscious urge to continue takes over the group and the "hum" of recitation resumes …' He later refers back to this vignette as 'the almost hypnotic sound created by constant multiple recitations of young voices punctuated by modelling from a deeper-voiced expert. The Qur'ān here becomes an audible facet of the environment' (p156). As a complete contrast to the artistry and sympathy displayed by Rosowsky in his field notes, see, for example, the acerbic references to Qur'anic memorisation and recitation by the American evangelist S M Zwemer (1867–1952) in his *Childhood in the Muslim World* (1915).

51 Obviously, different mosques and teachers will arrange the time over the week to include such foci and, undoubtedly, this will vary across different cultural and Islamic traditions. It would be interesting to gather and analyse material on this eg contrasting practice in a Deobandi-influenced mosque such as Balfour Road, Ilford, and another mosque affected by Somali traditions (Somalis having a strong reputation for their quality of Qur'anic memorisation).

52 It has been estimated that pious Muslims who observe all five formal prayers (*salah*) during the day will repeat the words of *surat ul-Fatihah* at least 17 times daily (Rosowsky 2008, p66).

53 The practice of taking the month of Ramadan as a holiday is clearly a long-established practice within Islam: see Makdisi (1981), p95. For the same practice being followed in a contemporary Pakistani madrasa, see Bano (2007).

54 Within the English state education system over the last 25 years or so (1992 marked the beginning of the Ofsted system through which mainstream schools came to have regular inspections), there have been constant exhortations to teachers to become more 'demanding' of their students and to make school work both 'rigorous' and 'challenging'.

55 Much of the work in this chapter was used or developed in a series of articles and book chapters: see Gent 2005, 2011b, 2013, 2015.

56 In some North African countries like Libya and Senegal, there has been the traditions of a student copying down the verses of the Qur'an on to a wooden tablet (*loh*), washing them off when memorised and then repeating the exercise with the next passage. See Eickelman (1978), p493 for the traditional method used in Moroccan religious schools. See also the following document: (http://www.saudiaramcoworld.com/issue/199105/learning.the.word.of.god.htm (accessed 29.8.11).

57 It is a common practice for those students who have already technically completed hifz to keep coming to hifz classes for another period—a year or more perhaps—in order to go through the memorised text again in order to make sure that it was firmly 'fixed' in their memory. Whilst observing a boys' hifz class at another mosque in October 2017, it was pointed out to me that two of the boys sitting in the class were doing just this.

58 The use of the word 'reverted' in this sense is a logical consequence of the doctrine of *fitrah*, the Qur'anic belief that 'human beings are created with a neutral state of purity (*fitrah*) that is subsequently formed by the individual and social realities of individuals' (Sahin 2013, p80). Thus, in 'converting' to Islam, a person 'reverts back' to his or her original state at birth.

59 *Surah Yasin* (Surah 36) has been called 'the heart of the Qur'an'. For an indication of the everyday seriousness with which it is regarded and used, see Malik 2011, p237: '... I am reading from the Holy Book now, standing by Dad's grave in Bradford. From Surah 36, which is called the Ya'Sin, also known as the Throbbing Heart of the Koran. The one you recite to ease the pain of the dead and to receive blessings for yourself'.

60 Within some families, traditions have developed down the generations of family members becoming *huffaz*: see Gent 2015.

61 For a powerful example of the impact of hearing Qur'anic recitation on a Muslim, take this example by Mohammad Akram Nadwi of his response to hearing the prayer leader's recitation of Surat al-Mulk (Surah 67, 'Supreme Power') during *fajr*, the first prayer of the day. This took place whilst Nadwi was a student in the Nadwat al-Ulama madrasah in northern India: 'His mode of Qur'anic recitation is majestic and full of pathos, his modulating voice adding much beauty … His recitation brought to mind the melody of birds, singing in ecstasy. There was a marked note, too, of pathos in his delivery. It emanated from the heart, as if overcome with joy after a long spell of sorrow. The rise and fall of his voice had a direct effect on my heart and mind. We felt as if the Qur'an was being revealed to us directly. His recitation seemed an inseparable part of the order of the universe. Our hearts were irresistibly drawn towards the Qur'anic message. It was akin to the absorption of rainwater by plants, which brings about their flourishing. Every object appeared to be in submission, in communion with the Divine. The dawn itself seemed to pause, to halt and seek the Lord's leave, to ask for illumination from that Divine Light before proceeding. We were immersed in the Qur'an recitation as if nothing else existed, as if all the vanity of the outer world had vanished, and only devout souls inhabited the earth. This spiritual experience helped us transcend our material constraints': Nadwi (2007), pp19, 20.

62 For an example, one of many available, of a non-Muslim profoundly moved by hearing the Qur'an being recited, note the following comment by the British orientalist, Arthur J Arberry. The scene was Cairo during the month of Ramadan whilst he was working on his famous translation of the Qur'an into English: 'I would sit on the veranda of my Gezira house and listen entranced to the old, white-beaded Sheykh who chanted the Koran for the pious delectation of my neighbour … It was then that I, the infidel, learnt to understand and react to the thrilling rhythms of the Koran, only to be apprehended when listened to at such a time in such a place': Arberry, A, *Koran Interpreted*, p18: cited in Moosa (2015), p63. Again, in his fascinating journal of life in Jerusalem between 1904–1946, Wasif Jawhariyyeh, famous story-teller and oud player, recalls many examples of when both he and his father (both Arab Orthodox Christians) were profoundly moved by hearing the Muslim call to prayer in Arabic, for instance: 'The window of the hall (the sitting room) of Dar al-Jawhariyyeh [the Jawhariyyeh family house] in Saadiyeh overlooked the red minaret, so we used to listen passionately to the muezzins who had good voices. When Sheikh Muhammad al-Silwani came from Egypt, he had graduated from Al-Azhar. He was a master of the *adhan* (call to prayer) and his vocal stretching skills were on

a par with those of the greatest musicians. God had blessed him with a beautiful voice, and my father used to wake me up to listen to his morning call to prayer' (Tamari & Nassar, 2014, pp88–89)

63 Note what Sikand (2005) has to say about the 'simple character' of madrasas in India: 'Teaching methods have remained largely unchanged over the centuries in most traditional madrasas... Blackboards are rarely used, except in junior classes' (p114). Compare this with what he later says of the Islamic International School in Mumbai in which 'Its brightly painted classrooms are equipped with blackboards, tables and chairs, and colourful posters decorate the walls' (p205).

64 Though students do clearly move on through Qur'anic memorisation at their own individual pace, this is not to suggest, of course, that individual students are not conscious of the pace of other students in the class and their own pace in relation to them. Note, for example, what a Muslim 16-year-old student, in a later piece of fieldwork (2016), said to me about the process of memorising a text within a group setting: 'it's kind of very hectic and pressuring in a way. Cos everyone else in the class is also going at the same speed as you and you want to compete with them in a way. And you don't really like falling behind or people going ahead of you'.

65 Note the manual of advice for students brought together by Al-Zarnuji (d602AH/1223CE) in which he exhorts students to remember that the night hours are a good time for study but particularly the period of dusk and the hour of dawn (al-Zarnuji, 2001, p19).

66 We can assume that there is some variety in the 'regime' that is run by particular teachers. In observing mosque classes at work over recent years, it has been my experience that a queue sometimes does not form as the teacher will call up individual students to the front when he is ready to hear that person read. As to the practice of calling up more than one student—one, two or even three, perhaps—and hearing them all read their own individual memorised section *simultaneously*, it would appear that there is an ongoing debate about whether this is appropriate. Some Muslims that I have discussed this with have expressed their amazement that some teachers seem to have the ability to point out corrections needed to each student, even though he is listening to a group reciting at the same time. Others, however, have frowned at the practice, saying that it is impossible to give the required attention to more than one student at a time.

67 In order to ensure that students undertaking hifz do so in the most efficient and effective manner, a number of different memorisation systems appear to have developed within the Muslim world. That employed in the maktab in question was, not surprisingly, using a method that is often found in groups associated with the Indian sub-continent. This consists of involving the students in a repeated cycle of three stages. Stage 1 (sometimes referred to as *sabaq*—the new 'lesson' for the day) involves students in learning a fresh piece of text which, when mastered, leads them on to the next stage. Stage 2 then consists of them revising the piece of text which had been memorised immediately before that learned at stage 1. When this has been revised and successfully recited from memory, stage 3 consists of revising a longer piece of text that had been memorised in the past. In that the Qur'an, with the exception of chapter 1 (*surat ul-Fatihah*, 'The Opener'), is organised from the longest to the shortest surahs, it is customary in this method to begin with memorising the shorter surahs which begin the last 30th section (*juz*) of the Qur'an. (There is, in fact, subtlety in this in that those now attempting hifz, will, as younger children, already have memorised some of the short surahs at the end of the Qur'an. So, their hifz 'journey', so to speak, builds upon solid ground.) The pattern of hifz classes then becomes based on these three stages. For example, when early morning hifz classes, are operating in addition to weekday evening classes, it is sometimes the practice to carry out stages 1 and 2 in the early morning session and then devote the evening session to stage 3. By contrast, a method developed in Turkey and the Balkans—referred to as 'memorising in circles'—consists of working through and memorising the last page of each of the 30 *juz* of the Qur'an, then the second from last page of each *juz*, as well as revising the previously memorised first page of each *juz*, and so on. This circular method of memorising the Qur'an is said to be particularly appropriate to hifz students who do not have Arabic as their native language and who cannot, therefore, link consecutive pages in their memory because of their meaning (Halilovich 2005, p75). See also, note 56 above.

68 *Dhur/dhor* is a word that means 'revision' in Urdu.

69 Note: 'The motives for learning the recitation of the Qur'an are mainly religious, but what is considered properly 'religious' in Islam embraces cultural, social, aesthetic, and other dimensions as well' (Denny 1989, p22).

70 The root *h-f-z* in Arabic carries a range of meanings: to guard, protect, take care of, watch, put in store, preserve. (Omar 2005, p129).

71 A Muslim scholar acquaintance of mine has expressed this memorably: 'When you want to talk to Allah, you make *du'a*: when you want Allah to talk to you, you read the Qur'an'.

72 Writing in 1836 on the manners and customs of 'modern' Egyptians, the British Orientalist, translator and lexicographer E W Lane (1801–1876) noted the following: 'All who are learning to read, recite or chant their lessons aloud, at the same time rocking their heads or bodies incessantly backwards and forwards; which practice is observed by all persons in reciting the Kur-án, being thought to assist the memory' (1978, p66). Ware (2014), in talking about the practice of rocking in West African Qur'anic schools, draws a musical analogy: 'They rock rhythmically as they recite, using their bodies as a pianist would use a metronome' (p9). For more on the practice of rocking whilst reciting or memorising, see also: St John (1845, p31), Rosowsky (2001, p68), Rosowsky (2008, p167), Malik (2011, p108).

73 Note: '[M]emorising the whole Qur'an is a task of some magnitude in terms of time, effort, and discipline, in comparison to the scope of memorisation in other traditions' (Boyle 2006, p491).

74 There is a well-known hadith which says that that which has been memorised 'can slip away from you more easily than camels can escape the cords with which they are hobbled' (Bukhari, *Sahih* VI, 238: cited in Robinson, 2003, 16). Compare: 'The process of memorisation of the Qur'an is expressly difficult and demanding, but it is even more difficult to save what is memorised from forgetfulness' (Halilovic 2005, p93).

75 See Gent 2011a.

76 The issue of whether the participation of Muslim students in supplementary schooling—as in mosque classes in general or hifz classes in particular, for example—has an impact on their mainstream schooling, and vice versa, continues to fascinate. There is no evidence that this has been researched at any great depth, however, though the work of Andrey Rosowsky in Literacy Studies has touched on this (see Rosowsky 2008 in particular) and occasional references to others sharing an interest in this issue can be found. See, for example, this reference in a report on the training and development of Muslim faith leaders published by the Department of Communities and Local Government in 2010:

'a teacher at a school in the Midlands informed the review team about research he had carried out whilst studying at the University of Birmingham in order to ascertain the impact of traditional teaching methods on academic progress. The majority of the students whom he interviewed felt that traditional methods involving extensive memorisation of chapters of the Qur'an and *hadith*, along with the ability to understand the finer points of *fiqh*, had developed their powers of memorisation and cognition which in turn helped them to do well in subjects of the National Curriculum' (DCLG 2010, p43). In March 2016, Bill Gent and Jenny Berglund (Södertörn University, Stockholm) carried out a research project at a secondary school in north-east London with the aim of finding out what Muslim students themselves believed to be the outcome in their own lives of participating in two traditions of education: that is, Muslim supplementary schooling and mainstream secular schooling. The results of this action research project are in the process of being published. In early 2018, these two researchers will be carrying out another similar research project but this time in an English primary school and with Muslim pupils of nine to ten years of age.

77 See note 76 above.

78 For more about the role and expectations of the hafiz within contemporary English Muslim society and beyond, see Gent 2016.

79 His role within the wider community has both continued and expanded to this day.

80 The notion of the embodiment of knowledge in general and of the Qur'an in particular has been familiar in both Islamic thinking and writing (see Gent, in press, and Ware 2014).

81 See Robson (2012) for a fascinating study of the place of memorising poetry and text within the US and Great Britain from the nineteenth century into the twentieth. The author notes that memorisation and recitation of poetry was a significant feature of the state elementary education system in Great Britain until the first part of the twentieth century (though slightly longer in the United States). But, she also notes that, 'The memorisation of poetry ... has not disappeared in either Britain or the United States, and it seems improbable that it will ever vanish completely; for a variety of different reasons, there will always be those in any given community who find this activity appealing and worthwhile,

and who will therefore practice it themselves and induce others to do likewise' (p4).

82 It is noteworthy that Robson (2012) judges that public attitudes to rote learning and memorisation are markedly different in Britain compared to the US: in the former, she detects a very 'conflicted response' associated with negative views of 'Victorian education' in general (p233)—whilst, in the latter, a much more relaxed and affirmative attitude.

83 See the excellent series of Tudor conspiracy novels by S J Parris (eg *Treachery*, 2014) in which Giordano Bruno (1548–1600) plays a leading role and there are occasional references to his reputation across Europe for creating devices to develop human memory.

84 In modern times, too, individuals with remarkable memory of recall have been identified, including: the historian and archaeologist, Vere Gordon Childe (see Bryson 2010, pp35, 37); the poet Coleridge (see Sachs 2017, pp112–114); and the Indian statesman, Jawaharlal Nehru (see Hahari 2015, p2).

85 Catherine Robson (2012, op cit), in her survey of the prominence of memorisation and recitation in English and American state schools in the nineteenth century and across into the twentieth, suggests a number of reasons why British classroom memorisation and recitation began to lose its dominance and stature within the classroom for example: the growing consensus in the twentieth century that memorisation without understanding was a pointless exercise (p78); the abolition of the elementary school system in the United Kingdom in 1944 in favour of a system the underlying social and educational ideas of which were markedly different from that which preceded it (p80); the growing gap between theory and practice (p78); and, the breaking of the link between funding and the recitational prowess of pupils. In addition, there were significant changes in pedagogy (the desire, for example, that pupils analyse and question as well as drawing on their own creative powers) and the growing practice of 'silent reading' (p81).

86 I was grateful to Robin Richardson for pointing out the importance of this distinction during the preparation of the original thesis.

87 Not only is the education scene in England increasingly complex (with the changing role of local [education] authorities and the growth of academies, for

instance) but it has also become increasingly clear how much education-speak is both prone to fashion and political exigencies and power. At the time that this thesis was written, as such, the concept of 'social cohesion' was in the ascendency and was inspiring some notable social projects. The concept—as well as that of—'multi-culturalism', for instance—has now fallen out of both linguistic fashion and political favour.

88 This finds a remarkable parallel in the critique of B V Street of the way in which literacy campaigns have been introduced into particular cultures and societies, whether the initiators have been from other societies or groups from within the same society (Street 1995).

89 See Gent (2012).

References

Abercrombie N, Hill S, Turner B S (2000), *The Penguin Dictionary of Sociology*, London, Penguin

Abdel-Haleem, M A S (2004) *The Qur'an* (Oxford: OUP)

Abu Guddah, A F (2003), *Prophet Muhammad the Teacher and His Teaching Methodologies*, Karachi, Zam Zam

Achebe, C (1963), *No Longer at Ease*, London, Heinemann

Alam, Arshad (2011) *Inside a Madrasa: Knowledge, Power & Islamic Identity in India* (New Delhi: Routledge)

Ali, A Y (1983), *The Holy Qur'an: Text, Translation and Commentary*, Brentwood US, Amana.

Al Raee, Mohammad Farooq Mohammad (2009) *The Practical Method of Learning & Teaching the Qur'ān: Its Memorization and Recitation, with Tajweed & Mastery*, Jeddah: Furqan group for Education & IT

Al-Sadan, I A (1999), 'The Pedagogy of the Prophet', *Muslim Educational Quarterly*, 16:2, pp5–18

Ansari, H (2004), *'The Infidel Within': Muslims in Britain Since 1800*, London, Hurst

Anwar, M (1979), *The Myth of Return: Pakistanis in Britain*, London, Heinemann

Armstrong, K (1991), *Muhammad: Biography of the Prophet*, London, Phoenix

Armstrong, K (2001), *Islam: A Short History*, London, Phoenix

Armstrong, K (2004), *The Spiral Staircase: A Memoir*, London, HarperCollins

Atkinson, R (1998), *The Life Story Interview*, Thousand Oaks Ca, Sage

Bano, M (2007) 'Beyond Politics': The Reality of a Deobandi Madrasa in Pakistan', *Journal of Islamic Studies*, 18:1, pp43–68)

Baumann, G (1996), *Contesting Culture: Discourses of Identity in Multi-Ethnic London*, Cambridge, Cambridge University Press

BBC Radio 4 (2004a), 'Who Controls Europe's Muslims?', broadcast 17.6.04 as part of the *Crossing Continents* series

BBC Radio 4 (2004b), *File on 4*, broadcast 20.7.04

BBC Radio 4 (2004c), 'Rookie Imams', broadcast 26.8.04

BBC Radio 4 (2004d), 'Muslim Teachers at Eton', broadcast 26.9.04

BBC Two (2005), 'Who Wants to be a Mullah?', broadcast 5.3.05

Becker, G S (1992), 'The Economic Way of Looking at Life', 1992 Nobel Lecture in Economics: http://nobelprize.org/economics/laureates/1992/index.html, accessed 2.1.05

Berger, P L & Hefner, R W (2003), 'Spiritual Capital in Comparative Perspective', Metanexus Institute Spiritual Capital Research Programme, www.metanexus.net/spiritual_capital/ accessed 2.1.05

Berglund, Jenny (2010) *Teaching Islam: Islamic Religious Education in Sweden* (Münster: Waxmann)

Berkey, Jonathan P(1992) *The Transmission of Knowledge in Medieval Cairo: A Social History of Islamic Education* (Princeton: Princeton University Press)

Bhatti, G (1999), *Asian Children at Home and at School: An Ethnographic Study*, London, Routledge

Birmingham Supplementary Schools Forum, www.bgfl.org/services/suppschl/, accessed May 2005

Bonino, Stefano (2017) *Muslims in Scotland: The Making of Community in a Post-9/11 World* (Edinburgh: Edinburgh University Press).

Bourdieu, P (1986), 'The Forms of Capital' in Robinson, J G (ed), *Handbook of Theory and Research for the Sociology of Education*, New York, Greenwood

Boyle, H (2004), *Quranic Schools: Agents of Preservation and Change*, New York, RoutledgeFalmer

Boyle, H (2006) 'Memorization & Learning in Islamic Schools', *Comparative Education Review*, 50:3, pp478–495

Bradbury, R (1976), *Fahrenheit 451*, London, Grafton

British Educational Research Association (BERA) (1992), *Ethical Guidelines*, www.bera.ac.uk, accessed April 2003

Bunt, G (2000), *Virtually Islamic: Computer-mediated Communication and Cyber Islamic Environments*, Cardiff, University of Wales Press

Buruma, I & Margalit, A (2004), *Occidentalism: A Short History of Anti-Westernism*, London, Atlantic

Buzan, T (2000), *The Mind Map Book*, London, BBC

Cantwell Smith, W (1971), 'The Study of Religion and the Study of the Bible', *Journal of the American Academy of Religion*, 39:2, pp131–140

Cantwell Smith, W (1980), 'The True Meaning of Scripture: An Empirical Historian's Nonreductionist Interpretation of the Qur'an', *International Journal of Middle East Studies*, 11:4, pp487–505

Cesari, J (2005), 'Mosque Conflicts in European Cities: Introduction', *Journal of Ethnic and Migration Studies*, 31:6, pp1015–1024

Clark, P (1986), *Marmaduke Pickthall: British Muslim*, London, Quartet

Coleman, J S (1988), 'Social capital in the Creation of Human Capital', *The American Journal of Sociology*, vol 94, Supplement: Organisations and Institutions: Sociological and Economic Approaches to the Analysis of Social Structure, S95–S120

Coles, Maurice Irfan (2008) *Every Muslim Child Matters: practical guidance for schools & children's services* (Stoke on Trent: Trentham)

Council on Islamic Education, www.cie.org: 'Education and the Rise of Universities in Muslim Lands and Europe', segment II of *Education and Scholarship* unit, pp81–87, accessed January 2004

Cush, D (2005), 'The Faith Schools Debate', *British Journal of Sociology of Religion*, 16:3, pp435–442

Department of Communities and Local Government (2010) *The training and development of Muslim Faith Leaders: Current practice and future possibilities* (London: DCLG Publications). www.communities.gov.uk/publications/communities/trainingmuslimleaderspractice

Denny, Frederick M (1989) 'Qur'an Recitation: A Tradition of Oral Performance', *Oral Tradition* 4:1–2, 5–26

Desforges, C (2005), 'Collaboration for Transformation: Why Bother?', DfES Standards Site, www.standards.dfes.gov.uk, accessed May 2005

DfES (2003), *Excellence and Enjoyment*, London, Department for Education and Skills

DfES (2003), *Aiming High: Raising the Achievement of Minority Ethnic Pupils*, London, Department for Education and Skills

DfES (2004), *Every Child Matters: Working with Voluntary Community Organisations to Deliver Change for Children and Young People*, London, Department for Education and Skills

DfES/NCSL (2005), *Primary Strategy Learning Networks*, London, Department for Education and Skills

Egan, K (undated), *Memory, Imagination and Learning: Connected by the Story*, http://www.educ.sfu.ca/kegan/MemoryIM.html, accessed 7.10.05

Eickelman, D F (1978), 'The Art of Memory: Islamic Education and Its Social Reproduction', *Comparative Studies in Society and History*, 20:4, pp485–516

Eickelman, D F (1985), *Knowledge and Power in Morocco: The Education of a Twentieth Century Notable*, Princeton, Princeton University Press

Erricker, C (2001), *From* 'Silence to Narration: A Report on the Research Method(s) of the Children and Worldviews' Project', *British Journal of Religious Education*, 23:3, pp156–164

Geaves, R (1996), *Sectarian Influences within Islam in Britain*, Leeds, University of Leeds

References

Geaves, Ron (2007) 'Twenty Years in Fieldwork: Reflections on Reflexivity in the Study of British Muslims' (University of Chester: Chester Academic Press)

Geaves, Ron (2010) *Islam in Victorian Britain: The Life and Times of Adbullah Quilliam* (Markfield, Leicestershire: Kube Publishing).

Geertz, C (1976), 'Art as a Cultural System', *Modern Language Notes*, 91:6, pp1473–1499

Gent, B (2005) 'Intercultural learning: Education and Islam—a case study' in Jackson & McKenna (eds), *Intercultural Education & Religious Plurality Oslo:* The Oslo Coalition on Freedom of Religion or Belief)

Gent, B (2006), 'The Educational Experiences of British Muslims: Some Life-Story Images', *Muslim Education Quarterly*, 23: 3&4, 33–42

Gent B (2011a) 'But You Can't retire as a *Hafiz*: fieldwork within a British *hifz* class', *Muslim Education Quarterly*, 24:1&2, 55–63

Gent B (2011b) 'The world of the British *hifz* class student: observations, findings & implications for education & further research', *British Journal of Religious Education*, 33:1, 3–15

Gent B (2013), 'Muslim Education and the *Hifz* Process: Some Images & Issues' in Miller J, O'Grady K & McKenna (Eds) *Religion in Education: Innovation in International Research* (New York & Abingdon: Routledge), 26–40

Gent, B (2015) '*Hifz* and *Huffaz* within the Islamic tradition: religious, cultural & educational considerations' in Parker, S G, Freathy, R J K , & Francis, L J (Eds) *History, Remembrance & Religious Education* (Oxford: Peter Lang), 341–363

Gent B (2016) 'The Hidden Olympians: the role of huffaz in the English Muslim community', *Contemporary Islam: Dynamics of Muslim Life*, 10:1.17–34. DOI 10.1007/s11562–014–0321-z

Gent B (in publication press) 'Traditional Islamic education & mainstream schooling in contemporary England: grasping the nature of the former & researching the relationship & interaction with the latter' in *European Perspectives on Islamic Education & Public Schooling* (Sheffield: Equinox)

Ghaffar, A (2001), 'Societal Problems and Education in Pakistan' in *Muslim Education Quarterly*, 19:1, p66

Gilliat-Ray, S (2005), 'Closed World: (Not) Assessing Deobandi *dar ul-uloom* in Britain', *Fieldwork in Religion*, 1:1, pp7–33

Gilliat-Ray (2006), 'Educating the 'Ulama: Centres of Islamic Religious Training in Britain', *Islam and Christian-Muslim Relations*, 17:1, pp55–76

Gilliat-Ray, Sophie (2010) *Muslims in Britain: An Introduction* (Cambridge: Cambridge University Press).Graham, W A (1985), 'Qur'an as Spoken Word' in Martin, R C (ed), *Approaches to Islam in Religious Studies*, Tucson, University of Arizona Press

Günther, S (2006) 'Be Masters in That You Teach and Continue to Learn: Medieval Muslim Thinkers on Educational Theory', *Comparative Education Review*, 50:3, pp367–388.

Halilovic, Safwat M (2005) *Hifz—Memorization of the Qur'an* (Dar al-Salam, Cairo). http://dc385.4shared.com/doc/MtnketZQ/preview.html (Accessed 3.10.11)

Halstead, J M (1995), 'Towards a Unified View of Islamic Education', *Islam and ChristianMuslim Relations*, 6:1, 1995, pp25–41

Hannon, V (2005), 'The future is Networked', DfES Standards Site, www.standards.dfes.gov.uk, accessed May 2005

Haque, M (2004), 'Review of the Progress of Muslim Education in the United Kingdom', *Muslim Education Quarterly*, 21:3 & 4, pp62–74

Hébert, Sun & Kowch (2004), 'Focusing on Children & Youth: The Role of Social Capital in Educational Outcomes in the Context of Immigration & Diversity', *Journal of International Migration & Integration*, 5:2, Spring 2004, pp229–249

Hirschkind, Charles (2001) 'The ethics of listening: cassette-sermon audition in contemporary Egypt'. *American Ethnologist*, 28:3, 623–649.

Hirschkind, Charles (2004) 'Hearing Modernity: Egypt, Islam, & the Pious Ear' in Veit Erlmann (Ed.) *Hearing Cultures: Essays on sound, listening & modernity*, 131–151 Oxford: Berg

Hirschkind, Charles (2006) *The Ethical Soundscape: Cassette Sermons & Islamic Counterpublics* (New York: Columbia University Press).Home Office (2005), *'Preventing Extremism Together': Report of Home Office Working Groups*, London, Home Office

Hopkins, D (2005), 'Every School a Great School: Meeting the Challenge of a Large Scale Long Term Educational Reform', London Centre for Leadership in Learning, Institute of Education, University of London, 30.6.05

Hussain, S (2004), 'An Introduction to Muslims in the British Census', paper presented at the Muslims in Britain Network, University of Birmingham, September 2004 IBERR (May 2001, second revised edition), *Manual for Muslim Schools*, IBERR, Cape Town, South Africa

Ilford Islamic Centre (2003), *Ilford Islamic Centre 25th Anniversary: 1978–2003*, Ilford

Ilford Muslim Society (1986/7), [no title], a booklet consisting of photographs, fund-raising appeal letter, ground plans and other documentation, distributed to aid fund-raising

Iannaccone, L R & Klick, J (2003), *Spiritual Capital: An Introduction and Literature Review*, Philadelphia USA, Metanexus Institute Spiritual Capital Research Programme, www.metanexus.net/spiritual_capital/, accessed 2.1.05

Jackson, D (2005), 'Five Reasons to Work with Other Schools', DfES Standards Site, www. standards.dfes.gov.uk, accessed May 2005

Jackson, R (1997), *Religious Education: An Interpretive Approach*, London, Hodder & Stoughton

Jackson, R (2000), 'The Warwick Religious Education Project: The Interpretive Approach to Religious Education' in Grimmitt, M (ed), *Pedagogies of Religious Education*, Great Wakering, McCrimmons

Jamiatul Ulama Transvaal Taalimi Board (1988a), *Akhlaaq and Aadaab made Easy*, Book 1

Jamiatul Ulama Transvaal Taalimi Board (1988b), *Akhlaaq and Aadaab made Easy*, Book 7

Jamiatul Ulama Transvaal Taalimi Board (1988c), *History Made Easy*, Book 2

Jamiatul Ulama Transvaal Taalimi Board (1988d), *Fiqh made Easy*, Book 1

Kane, C H (1972), *Ambiguous Adventure*, Oxford, Heinemann Educational

Kirklees Council, West Yorkshire, Madressahs and Supplementary Schools Project, www. kirklees.gov.uk/community/health-care/childrenandfamilies/parentsupport/madressahs.shtml, accessed May 2005

Knott, Kim (2009) 'How to study religion in the modern world' in Woodhead, L, Kawanami, H & Partridge, C *Religions in the Modern World: Traditions and Transformations* (London: Routledge)

Kvale, Steinar (1996), *Interviews: An Introduction to Qualitative Research Interviewing*, (London & Thousand Oaks, Ca: Sage Publications)

Kureishi, H (2004), *My Ear at His Heart: Reading My Father*, London, Faber and Faber

Lane, E W (1978) *Manners and Customs of the Modern Egyptians* (The Hague & London: East-West Publications)

Lawson, I (2005a), *Leading Islamic Schools in the UK: A Challenge for Us All*, Nottingham, National College for School Leadership

Lawson, I (2005b), *Leading Islamic Schools in the UK: A challenge for Us All*, Research Summary, Nottingham, National College for School Leadership

LeBor, A (1997), *A Heart Turned East: Among the Muslims of Europe and America*, London, Little, Brown and Company

Lewis, P (2002, 2nd ed), *Islamic Britain: Religion, Politics and Identity among British Muslims*, London, I B Tauris

Lewis, P (2004), 'New Social Roles and Changing Patterns of Authority amongst British *'ulamā'*, *Archives de Sciences Sociales des Religions*, 125, pp169–188

Lewis, Philip (2007) *Young, British and Muslim* (London: Continuum)

Lieberman, A (1999), 'Networks', *Journal of Staff Development*, 20:3

London Borough of Redbridge (2005), *Borough Profile*

Lumley, J (2004), *No Room for Secrets*, London, Michael Joseph

Makdisi, George (1981) *The Rise of Colleges: Institutions of Learning in Islam and the West* (Edinburgh: Edinburgh University Press)

Malik, I H (2004), *Islam and Modernity: Muslims in Europe and the United States*, London, Pluto

Malik, Zaiba (2011) *We Are a Muslim, Please* (London: Windmill Books)

Manchester City Council, Education Diversity and Inclusion Team, Supplementary Schools, www.manchester.gov.uk/education/diversity/supp_schools/, accessed May 2005

Manguel, A (1997), *A History of Reading*, London, Flamingo

Martin, P, Bhatt, A, Bhojani, N, Creese, A (2003), *A Preliminary Report on a Survey of Complementary Schools and Their Communities in Leicester*, Leicester, University of Leicester School of Education

Martin, P, Creese, A, Bhatt, A, Bhojani, N, (2004), *A Final Report on Complementary Schools and their Communities in Leicester*, Leicester, University of Leicester School of Education McCarthy, H, Miller, P, Skidmore, P (2004), *Network Logic*, London, Demos: www.demos.co.uk, accessed May 2005

Mattson, Ingrid (2008) *The Story of the Qur'an: Its History and Place in Muslim Life* (Malden, MA: Blackwell Publishing).

Mogra, I (2004), '*Makatib* Education in Britain: A Review of Trends and Some Suggestions for Policy', *Muslim Education Quarterly*, 21:3 & 4, pp19–27

Moosa, Ebrahim (2015), *What is a Madrasa?* (Edinburgh, Edinburgh University Press)

Mortel, R (1997), 'Madrasas in Mecca During the Medieval Period: a Descriptive Study Based on Literary Sources', *Bulletin of the School of Oriental and African Studies*, 60:2, pp236–252

Muslim Parliament of Great Britain (2006), *Child Protection in Faith-Based Environments: A Guideline Report*

Muslim Public Affairs Committee UK (MPACUK), www.mpacuk.org, accessed April 2006

Nadwi, Mohammad Akram (2007) *Madrasah Life: A student's day at Nadwat al-ulama*, (London: Turath)

Nelson K (2001; first published 1985), *The Art of Reciting the Qur'an*, Cairo, American University in Cairo

Nesbitt, E (1993), 'Photographing Worship: Ethnographic Study of Children's Participation in Acts of Worship', *Visual Anthropology*, Vol 5, pp285–306

Nesbitt, E (2001), 'Ethnographic Research at Warwick', *British Journal of Religious Education*, 23:3, pp144–155

Nesbitt, E (2003), *Interfaith Pilgrims: Living Truths and Truthful Living*, London, Quaker Books

Nesbitt, E (2004), *Intercultural Education: Ethnographic and Religious Approaches*, Brighton, Sussex Academic Press

Nielsen, J (1995, 2nd ed), *Muslims in Western Europe*, Edinburgh, Edinburgh University Press

Nofal, Nabil (1993) 'Al-Ghazali (AD 1058–111; AH 450–505), *Prospects: the quarterly review of comparative education*, XXIII: 3/4, 519–542.

Norman, W R (1991), 'Photography as a Research Tool', *Visual Anthropology*, 4, pp193–216

Office for National Statistics, www.statistics.gov.uk, 'Selection of Interesting and Frequently Requested Indicators' for Redbridge, accessed December 2003.

Omar, Abdul Mannan (2005) *Dictionary of The Holy Qur'an* (Hockessin, USA: Noor Foundational International)

Ong, W J (1982), *Orality and Literacy: The Technologizing of the Word*, London, Methuen

Østberg, S (2003), *Pakistani Children in Norway: Islamic Nurture in a Secular Context*, Leeds, University of Leeds

Paigaam 'Eighty Two Years Old Memorizes the Qur'an', *Paigaam*, issue 145, April 2005 (www.imws. org.uk/paigaamhome.htm)

Parker-Jenkins, M (1995), *Children of Islam: A Teacher's Guide to Meeting the Needs of Muslim Pupils*, Stoke-on-Trent, Trentham

Plummer, K (2001), *Documents of Life 2*, London, Sage

Portelli, A (1997), *The Battle of Valle Giulia: Oral History and the Art of Dialogue*, Madison, University of Wisconsin Press

Portes, A (1998), 'Social Capital: Its Origins and Applications in Modern Sociology', *Annual Review of Sociology*, 24, 1–24

Putnam, R (2001), *Bowling Alone: The Collapse and Revival of American Community*, New York, Simon & Schuster

Ramadan, T (2004), *Western Muslims and the Future of Islam*, Oxford, Oxford University Press

Ramadan, Tariq (2008) *The Messenger: The Meanings of the Life of Muhammad* (London: Penguin)

Raza, M S (1991), *Islam in Britain: Past, Present and the Future*, Leicester, Volcano Press

Redbridge SACRE (2003), *Muslim Madrasahs in Redbridge*, London, Borough of Redbridge

Ritchie, D A (2003, 2nd ed), *Doing Oral History: A Practical Guide*, Oxford, Oxford University Press

Robinson, F (1999), 'Knowledge, its Transmission, and the Making of Muslim Societies' in *The Cambridge Illustrated History of the Islamic World*, pp208–249

Robinson, N (2003). *Discovering the Qur'ān: A Contemporary Approach to a Veiled Text*. London: SCM Press.

Robson, C (1993), *Real World Research: A Resource for Social Scientists and PractitionerResearchers*, Oxford, Blackwell

Rosenthal, Franz (2007) *Knowledge Triumphant: The Concept of Knowledge in Medieval Islam* (Leiden: Brill)

Rosowsky, A (2001) 'Decoding as a cultural practice and its effects on the reading process of bilingual pupils' in *Language and Education* 15:1, pp56–70

Rosowsky, A (2008) *Heavenly Readings: Liturgical Literacy in a Multilingual Context* (Bristol: Multilingual Matters)

Rosowsky, Andrey (2010) '"Writing it in English": script choices among young multilingual Muslims in the UK', *Journal of Multilingual & Multicultural Development*, 31:2, 163–179

Rosowsky, Andrey (2016) 'Heavenly enxtextualisation: the acquisition & performance of classical religious texts' in Lytra, V, Volk, D, & Gregory, Eve (eds) (2016) *Navigating Languages, Literacies & Identities: Religion in Young Lives*, 139–162

Runnymede Trust, The (1997), *Islamophobia: A Challenge For Us All*, London.

Russell, I (2006), 'Working *with* Tradition: Towards a Partnership Model of Fieldwork', *Folklore*, 117, pp15–32

Ruthven, M (1984), *Islam in the World*, London, Penguin.

Sahin, Abdullah (2013) *New Directions in Islamic Education: Pedagogy & Identity Formation*, Markfield: Kube Publishing

Said, E W (1997, 2nd ed), *Covering Islam: How the Media and the Experts Determine How We See the Rest of the World*, London, Vintage

Sardar, Ziauddin (2011) *Reading the Qur'ān* (London: Hurst & Co)

Sarwar, Mohammad (2016) *My Remarkable Journey: The Autobiography of Britain's first Muslim MP* (Edinburgh: Birlinn)

Sells, M (1999/2007), *Approaching the Qur'an: The Early Revelations*, Oregon, White Cloud Press

Shaw, A (2000), *Kinship and Continuity: Pakistani Families in Britain*, Amsterdam, HAP

Sherif, M A (2004), *Searching for Solace: A Biography of Abdullah Yusuf Ali, Interpreter of the Qur'an*, New Delhi, Adam

Sikand, Yoginder (2005) *Bastions of the Believers: Madrasas and Islamic Education in India* (New Delhi: Penguin).Smalley, S (2005), 'Teaching about Islam and Learning about Muslims: Islamophobia in the Classroom, *Resource*, 27:2, pp4–7

Smith, A (1998), *Accelerated Learning in Practice*, Stafford, Network Educational Press

Smith, G (2005), *Children's Perspectives on Believing and Belonging*, London, National Children's Bureau/Joseph Rowntree Foundation

St John, James Augustus (1845) *Egypt and Nubia, their scenery and their people, Being incidents of history and travel, from the best and most recent authorities, including J L Burckhardt and Lord Lindsay* (London: Chapman & Hall).

Suleiman, Y et al (2009) *Contextualising Islam in Britain: Exploratory Perspectives* (Cambridge: University of Cambridge)

Supplementary Schools Network, www.supplementaryschools.org.uk, accessed May 2005

TES (*Times Educational Supplement*) (2005), 'Fighting Freda', *Friday* supplement, 13.5.05

The Times (10.12.08), 'Teachers "beat and abuse" children at many Koran classes in Britain'

Thompson, P (2000, 3rd ed), *The Voice of the Past: Oral History*, Oxford, Oxford University Press

Ware, Rudolph T III (2014) *The Walking Qur'ān: Islamic Education, Embodied Knowledge, & History in West Africa* (Chapel Hill: University of North Carolina Press).

Watt, M (trans) (1994, 2nd ed), *The Faith and Practice of Al-Ghazali*, Oxford, Oneworld

Wohlstetter, P et al (2003), 'Improving Schools Through Networks: A New Approach to Urban School Reform', *Educational Policy*, 17:4, pp399–430

Yates, F A (1966), *The Art of Memory*, London, Ark

Zohar, D & Marshall I (2004), *Spiritual Capital: Wealth We Can Live By*, London, Bloomsbury

Appendices

Appendix 1

Balfour Road Mosque hifz class fieldwork: general checklist used for observations (see 3.5)

- ❏ Beginnings and endings
- ❏ Different types of activity and how distributed across a lesson (eg independent learning, meeting with teacher, working in pairs)
- ❏ The sequence of activities in a lesson
- ❏ Physical layout of room
- ❏ Appearance of teacher and students
- ❏ Spatial distribution of teacher and students
- ❏ Methods of teaching and learning
- ❏ Teaching aids used
- ❏ Physical movements and activities
- ❏ Sounds
- ❏ Atmosphere
- ❏ Protocols and conventions (adab)
- ❏ Interactions between students and between teacher and students

Could it be that this list can be refined during the course of the observations? or first observation used to gain general bearing and then subsequent observations used to focus on particular elements.

Appendix 2

Balfour Road Mosque hifz class fieldwork: example of ground plan annotated during an observation session (see 3.5 & 6.4)

Session 3

Monday 5.7.04 6.00 – 7.00 pm	Observation of hifz class. Further discussion with *name of student*	One hour

Physical positioning (@ 6.00 pm)

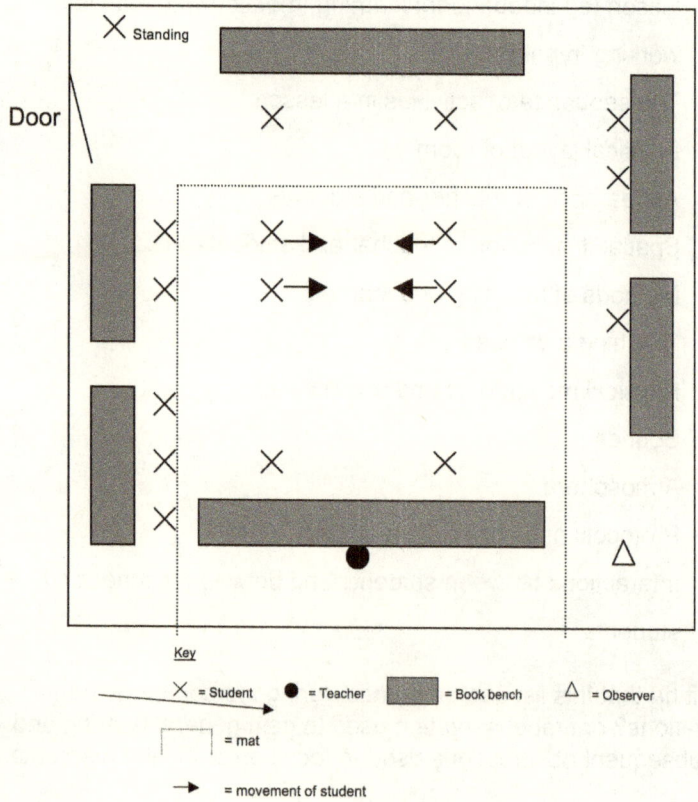

Appendix 3

Balfour Road Mosque hifz class fieldwork: interview schedule designed for use in interviewing students (see 3.5)

Experience as a hifz student
- Reasons for wanting to learn the Qur'an by heart
- Balance between their own and other people's choice/ pressure
- Why memorising the words and sounds of the Qur'an is important (and how they respond to the suggestion that, because books and CDRoms etc are available, there is no point in memorising the Qur'an any more)
- Methods that they use to memorise the Qur'an (and extent to which they have been taught/shown these)
- What it feels like when they are memorising the Qur'an
- What it feels like when they do a correct recitation
- What it feels like when they hear someone else (famous reciter?) recite the Qur'an
- What the qualities of a good hifz student are
- What the qualities of a good hifz teacher are
- What the atmosphere in the hifz class is like
- What is taking place in the photographs (both outwardly and inwardly)
- Best thing and worst thing about being in the hifz class
- What they will do when they become a hafiz
- How their family feels about them being in the hifz class

Experiences as a hifz student in relationship to the rest of their lives and experiences
- Whether being a hifz student make them feel different from other (a) Muslim people of their own age, (b) non-Muslim people of their own age
- Extent to which the time they spend in hifz activities has an effect on the rest of their lives (things they can and can't do etc)
- What happens when there is a clash of priorities (eg homework for school or work for hifz class; work for hifz class and going out with friends)

- Whether being a hifz student has an effect on their work at school or college (eg tiredness, better concentration, attitude to teachers, attitudes to learning, confidence in speaking, ability to listen)
- Whether how they learn in hifz class affects how they learn in school (and vice versa)
- Whether their capacity to memorise (the Qur'an) means that they can easily memorise other things (examples?)
- Whether they behave and act differently in hifz class and school
- Whether a Muslim adult could be both a hifz class teacher and a teacher in an LEA school
- Whether they think of both hifz class and classes as school as 'education'
- Any method of teaching and learning that takes place in school that could be use in the hifz class (and vice versa)
- If they had to choose between going to hifz class and school, which they would choose and why

General reflections
- Whether how Muslim children are taught in British mosques should change and reasons
- Their response to idea that teachers in mosques and teachers in schools should work more closely together

Appendix 4

Balfour Road Mosque hifz class fieldwork: information sheet devised to record information about individual students (see 3.5)

Information	Further notes
Name	
DoB / Age (Y & M)	
Family background	
How long in hifz class (Y & M)	
Time spent in hifz class in a typical week (timings + hrs) 　　　　　　　　　AM　　　　　　　PM Monday Tuesday Wednesday Thursday Friday Saturday Sunday	
Time spent in other hifz-related activities 　　　　　　　　　AM　　　　　　　PM Monday Tuesday Wednesday Thursday Friday Saturday Sunday	
School/educational background	

Appendix 5

Outside views of Balfour Road Mosque and associated buildings (see 5.2 & 6.4)

Appendix

Appendix 6

Photographs of the hifz class at work used as a promoptt during interviews (see 3.6)

Appendix 7

The routines and rhythms of the boys' hifz class (see 6.4)

www.ingramcontent.com/pod-product-compliance
Lightning Source LLC
Chambersburg PA
CBHW032254150426
43195CB00008BA/453